COMMUNICATION SKILLS
FOR THE
HELPING PROFESSIONS

COMMUNICATION SKILLS
FOR THE
HELPING PROFESSIONS

By

DAN W. EDWARDS
Ph.D., A.C.S.W., F.I.C.

School of Social Welfare
Louisiana State University
Baton Rouge, Louisiana

CHARLES C THOMAS • PUBLISHER
Springfield • Illinois • U.S.A.

Published and Distributed Throughout the World by

CHARLES C THOMAS • PUBLISHER

2600 South First Street

Springfield, Illinois, 62717, U.S.A.

© *1983 by* CHARLES C THOMAS • PUBLISHER

ISBN 0-398-04766-9

Library of Congress Catalog Card Number: 82-10799

With THOMAS BOOKS *careful attention is given to all details of manufacturing and
design. It is the Publisher's desire to present books that are satisfactory as to their physical
qualities and artistic possibilities and appropriate for their particular use.* THOMAS
BOOKS *will be true to those laws of quality that assure a good name and good will.*

Printed in the United States of America
CU-R-1

Library of Congress Cataloging in Publication Data

Edwards, Dan W
    Communication skills for the helping professions.

    Includes index.
    1. Communication in social work.   I. Title.
HV41.E34   1983   001.54'2'024362   82-10799
ISBN 0-398-04766-9

To my wife, Janet Jo,
who is a constant source
of positive inspiration and support

PREFACE

A NY client who comes to a helping professional, for whatever, reason, deserves to be looked at with the broadest kind of vision. Of all the technical aids that increase the helping professional's power of observation, none comes even close in value to the verbalized and nonverbalized communication that occurs between the therapist or counselor and client. Throughout all of the helping professions, communication remains a key element in both diagnosis and treatment. Communication is the most powerful resource available to all helping professionals.

For these reasons, the art and science of communicating with clients deserve continued study and development. The relationship between the helping professional and the client is directly based upon the talk that goes on between them. Unfortunately, even though a number of books have been written on communication skills in the helping professions, none has presented in a single volume the key elements of these skills for use with adults as well as children. Perhaps even more important, is that no book of this nature has offered special chapters on communication skills with children who are not old enough to talk, with the aged, as well as the unique skills necessary for communication with the retarded. It is to this end that the author attempted to put together a highly readable and usable book for social workers, counselors, therapists, nurses, and other members of the helping professions.

DWE

CONTENTS

COMMUNICATION SKILLS
FOR THE
HELPING PROFESSIONS

SECTION I

CHILDREN AND ADOLESCENTS

Chapter 1

BASIC FUNDAMENTALS OF COMMUNICATING WITH CLIENTS

INTRODUCTION

THE kind of verbal interaction and relationship between helping professionals and their clients should and does differ markedly from ordinary day-to-day communication and relationships among people. It may be true that some people obtain temporary relief and emotional reassurance by talking with a friend, relative, or perhaps a bartender. However, it is rather unlikely that any relief or change that results from this kind of communication is likely to be very lasting or permanent.

One way in which the communication between helping professionals and clients is unique rests upon the fact that one person is present to talk about himself or herself in order to receive some kind of help. The other person, the helping professional, is present to enable the client to communicate about himself or herself in a manner that will facilitate identification of the problem and lead to the development of a therapeutic relationship.

However, the specific interventive strategy to be utilized by the helping professional will be primarily dependent upon his or her particular theoretical frame of reference. However, this book is not intended to present an overview or a specific theory of counseling and/or psychotherapy. Nonetheless, there are certain principles, techniques, and fundamentals of interviewing or therapeutic communication that enhance understanding, problem identification, and the development of therapeutic helping relationship. To this end, this chapter attempts to present certain basic fundamentals of communication skills with clients.

PURPOSE AND OBJECTIVES

One of the first things that should be done when communicating with clients is to have a purpose clearly in mind. More specifically, one should have some notion of what is to be accomplished during the session, for example problem identification, ego support, and modification of a specific behavior.

Accordingly, a number of factors contribute to determining the purpose of communicating with a client. One of the most important factors is determined by the mission of the agency or institution for which you work, or the type of practice in which you are engaged. Other pertinent factors include whether or not this is to be your first session with the client, the middle, or the end of the therapeutic relationship, as well as the particular theoretical frame of reference, for example behavior modification and rational emotive therapy, that you use to guide your intervention strategy.

Nonetheless, each time you talk with a client, you should have a clear purpose in mind. Also, you should mutually clarify and develop objectives for each session with your client, always remaining flexible enough to make necessary changes when so indicated. All of this means that a great deal of skill is required for successful communication with clients.

BASIC CONSIDERATIONS AND FUNDAMENTALS

There are a number of basic considerations and technical points that can be offered to make communication with clients more successful. Many of these are obvious and well known, but some are not.

One of the first considerations in communicating with clients is to determine how long you wish to talk with them. I have found that most adult clients are able to remain attentive and actively participate for approximately one hour. Usually, though, I limit sessions to fifty minutes to permit time for making a few notes, and to prepare for the next client. However, young children tend to tire and lose attentiveness within thirty or forty minutes. This varies from one youngster to another, but should be kept clearly in mind.

Another not so obvious consideration is to make use of facial expressions and eyes of clients. A skilled clinician is constantly observing the client's face and eyes for subtle signs of distress, for example anxiety, anger, sadness, boredom, and distress. These observations aid the therapist in identifying and assessing feelings that may be present, but masked by the client's effort to appear calm. Further indications may be picked up by observing the client's walk, hand movements, and the way he or she sits or stands. Accordingly, personal appearance and the client's manner of dress can be very revealing. For example I distinctly recall a very depressed middle-aged woman who progressed from being totally unkempt to wearing a new hair style and bright crisp clothing, almost at the same pace with which she worked through her depression. However, none of these things can indicate anything unless they are carefully observed.

Still another aid in communicating with clients is practicing good listening skills. Sometimes you can learn more by listening than by talking. Also, it is just as helpful to pay attention to what is not being said as well as listening to what the client does say. This is the primary reason for communication: Help the client talk about himself or herself to listen and hear what is being said.

However, the client cannot communicate while the therapist is talking, so the less said, the better. However, this is not always as easy as it may sound. With some clients, just getting them to talk can be a major accomplishment.

Moreover, simply asking a client to tell you about himself or herself, and then sitting back to listen is not sufficient. Some clients have more difficulty talking openly about themselves than do others, and consequently require a good deal more prompting to be able to do so. Conversely, others talk freely, but may move from one subject to another so abruptly and frequently as to require constant direction and structure by the therapist in order to make sense.

Worse still, are those therapists who enjoy talking so much that they do not give the client much opportunity to talk about themselves. Another serious characteristic among some clinicians is to interrupt when something is being said that they may not particularly wish to hear. In doing this, the interfering therapist unwittingly tends to assume control, to move away from the topic, and to do so without awareness of what they have done.

I remember a young social worker who was sent to talk with a patient in the hospital. She returned to the office in less than fifteen minutes and asked if I would like to join her for a cup of coffee. When I asked her how the interview had gone, she explained that there was nothing of particular significance to talk about. She had overlooked completely that not only had the patient undergone serious surgery, her brother had been killed in an accident the day before. While we were drinking our coffee, she voluntarily brought up the subject of her brother having been killed in an accident approximately two years ago. Suddenly, by merely listening before talking, I was able to understand why her session with the patient was so brief. Specifically, she had not yet worked through her feelings about her own brother's death, and the recent similar problem of the patient was too painful to talk about. Fortunately, after helping her to realize what had happened, this assignment proved to be very helpful for the patient as well as herself.

Nonetheless, good listening skills do require an occasional indication from the therapist that he or she heard what was said, and that it was understood. This may be accomplished by illuminating on something the client has said, asking a question relevant to what was said, and by making occasional brief comments, for example "I can imagine how that made you feel," or "I see what you mean." However, the therapist must also learn to adjust the frequency of such brief indications to effectively correspond with the client's flow of communication.

Another important fundamental is to avoid becoming argumentative with the client, and feeling compelled to give advice, or to offer ingenious interpretations. It is best for the therapist to not make any interpretation until he or she and the client both have developed a good deal of awareness or insight about the particular problem.

The skillful use of open-ended questions usually elicits more information than do straightforward questions. For example you might say something like, "And after that?", "Before then, what?", "And?" Also, it is helpful to avoid questions that require only a simple yes or no answer, or those kinds of questions that tend to speak for the client, for example "Did it make you angry?" Rather, it would be better to ask, "And how did that make you feel?" This style of questioning permits the client to express his or her true feelings, rather than being obliged to agree with the therapist's guess.

Communication with clients is further enhanced when the therapist is precise and clear in what he or she says. This is especially important when making assignments and giving instructions. In essence, the important thing is for therapists to make certain their clients clearly understand what is said as well as what is expected of them.

It is not uncommon for clients to interpret very differently that which was intended by the therapist. For this reason, it is important to not hesitate in requesting clients to explain what they heard being said. Then, if the client misinterpreted what was intended, the therapist can clarify the meaning of the communication. Remember, any instructions worth giving are deserving of the little amount of time that may be required for the therapist to clarify the intended meaning.

I remember one specific case in point that clearly illustrates the importance of making certain that clients correctly interpret instructions. Namely, the mother of a young child who constantly set fires was instructed to reward the youngster for not playing with matches, to ignore talking about fire, and to keep matches out of the child's reach. A week later, the mother returned and said, "I tried what you suggested and it is really working." Her therapist responded with verbal praise. Unfortunately, not only had the mother misinterpreted the instructions, the therapist unwittingly positively reinforced the mother's act of tying the child to a chair and burning each of his fingers with a box of kitchen matches he had been caught with.

Conversely, it is just as important for the therapist to make certain he or she understands what is intended by the client. Nothing should be taken for granted. For example I remember a young psychology student who asked a client how much alcohol he usually drank. The client responded that he didn't really drink very much at all, only a few glasses of wine now and then. What the student neglected to determine was that "a little wine" to this client amounted anywhere from five to ten gallons a week. Whenever a client suggests that he or she "drinks a little," "worries a little," and so on, it should be clarified by the therapist until it can be translated into meaningful terms.

The client's right to confidentiality is another extremely

important fundamental worthy of mention. It should be emphasized, though, that this is the client's right or privilege rather than that of the therapist. More specifically, clients should have the assurance that what they confide in the helping professional will not be repeated to others without their express permission. Accordingly, clients have other rights as well, and the majority of agencies and institutions have these spelled out in written form to be explained to clients upon their first visit. It is not uncommon for many agencies and institutions to request clients to sign a form indicating that they have received a copy of the "Client's Bill of Rights" and understand them.

Awareness of self is an important and commonly accepted fundamental in effective therapeutic communication. However, this fundamental refers to the helping professional's awareness of his or her own prejudices and bias. This requires the therapist to not only be aware, but also to possess the strength to be honest with himself about these matters. There are a number of ways for helping professionals to continue developing self-awareness. Conferences with supervisors, value clarification groups, self-examination, and feedback from others are all helpful resources for helping professionals to develop self-awareness. Nevertheless, this is something that requires continuous assessment; as the therapist grows and changes, so do his or her values and attitudes. In so doing, helping professionals increase their skill in not projecting their values on their clients. Self-awareness can also broaden the range of human problems in which the therapist can more comfortably and effectively intervene.

Other important fundamentals in communicating with clients include looking for and recognizing incongruities, gaps, abrupt changes of subjects, and the first and last statements in client communications. More specifically, all of these things can be very revealing of what the client is feeling and thinking. Therefore, the skilled therapist always follows up when he or she recognizes one of these occurrences and has reason to suspect that it may be important.

Obviously, there are other fundamentals and techniques that may be helpful to some therapists in more effectively communicating with clients. However, these were not discussed either because they were so obvious or because they appear to be suitable for some but not for others. Undoubtedly, each helping professional will study all available techniques and adopt those that appear to be most suitable for himself or herself. Also, each therapist will wish to continue learning pertinent factors about certain age groups and human problems and behavior that will facilitate more effective communication with their clients. To this end, the remainder of this book was written.

Chapter 2

THE PREVERBAL CHILD

NEWBORN TO TWO

COMMUNICATION skills with infants and children who have not yet learned to talk have been sorely neglected in the literature of the helping professions. This is primarily so because children of this age have traditionally been thought of as more appropriately being within the purview of the psychiatrist or psychologist. Nonetheless, every family seen by any helping professional has at one time or another had a child who was in this age group.

It is not uncommon to hear students as well as seasoned practitioners express more concern and anxiety about how to relate to a child who is this age than anything else. As a result, it is also not uncommon for preverbal children to be excluded from family sessions or totally ignored. For these reasons, among others, this chapter was included.

Ordinarily, during the first two years of life, no talking is possible. Nevertheless, the helping professional should feel free to talk to the child as much as he or she wishes, because even though the child may not understand the words, he or she apparently derives some meaning from being spoken to.

On the other hand, in the place of words, children of this age do use and understand a nonverbal form of communication. The infant or child is able to sense and to attach meaning to every move and gesture an adult makes. This acute perception appears to be a basic characteristic of the youngster who is unable to talk or to understand the talk of others, but in a sharply responsive way is able to sense a

13

great deal of the things that go on around him or her. This responsiveness and perception may not always be accurate, but is always active, and practically every move or sound made in their presence has significance to them.

The significance that a child attaches to movement and speech is of a special nature. It differs from the meaning that an adult would attach to it. There is really no way of accurately determining the specific meaning of a preverbal child's interpretations. All that is known is (1) perceptions are obviously made, (2) reactions to them do occur and (3) both the meaning of the perceptions and the kind of reactions differ at different ages. Children in sizing up what they see and hear naturally do so from a very limited viewpoint. This is because they have such an infinitely small experience from which to draw similarities and conclusions that their perceptions and responses are narrowly centered on themselves and on their mother. In essence, this is the only world the child knows.

Children sense their own needs beginning with the first day of life, and they respond to them by nursing, wetting, crying, sleeping, and so forth. At first, that is the entirety of life. Very soon, however, the child adds to these inner perceptions of a rapidly growing attention and responds to this or her mother's or surrogate's every mood and move, sometimes recognizing changes in her even more surely than the mother does herself. Fortunately, most mothers soon learn to interpret fairly accurately, although not fully, most of the infant's messages.

However, something very exciting usually occurs around the age of two months. The infant, in addition to the reflex smile that occurs in response to pleasurable physical stimulation, suddenly begins to smile when the mother or surrogate merely becomes visible. What does this mean? Every mother, father, and grandparent can tell you that this is the first time the child is aware of and able to center his attention and senses on someone other than himself or herself. In essence, the child has made his or her first human connection and is beginning to interact in a social manner.

During the next few phases of development, the child begins to develop greater senses of differentiation for things and people around him or her. Meanwhile, physical development continues and is played out through constant moving about, pulling up, and carelessly exploring things in the world around them. These are the days of broken ash trays, lamps, and other such objects that were previously left unnoticed, and for awhile remained out of reach.

Of particular interest to the therapist is that although the child learns very early to understand his or her mother's behavior and the behavior of others who are frequently around him or her, this is not so for strangers. More specifically, the child has only one feeling about strangers: Strangers are potentially dangerous. Moreover, to the very young child everything strange, particularly anything suddenly strange, is likely to be perceived as being threatening and may result in the child becoming very fearful.

For this reason, making contact with very young children whom you have never been around is very much like chasing butterflies. Think back, if you will, about your early life experiences when you chased butterflies. The more you chased the more they would stay just beyond your reach. However, when you became tired or gave up and sat down, the butterfly would actually light on your arm or shoulder.

For very young children, there is no such thing as a friendly stranger or a pleasant sudden move. These things are all perceived as being potentially dangerous until proven to be otherwise. However, this same sudden move or sudden noise, if repeated several times, may very well lose its dangerous meaning. Familiarity enables the young child to come to accept such as part of his or her normal surroundings.

More specifically, each child in each situation should be given ample time to develop a sense of familiarity. This is particularly true of the very young child's relationship to a helping professional when they first meet. However, it should be pointed out again that the very young infant does not recognize clearly the differences in people, and as long as you are gentle, he or she does not regard you as dangerous. Again, this suspicion will continue until familiarity with the new person overtakes and replaces the strangeness.

In view of the suspicious, on-guard manner in which infants react to new people, perhaps the most effective approach to him or her is an indirect, almost passive one. If the therapist remains quiet and still, standing only close enough so that his or her presence is clearly noticeable, and if no threatening gestures are made, the child will have a good opportunity to look the helping professional over from what may be considered a safe position. This approach may be enhanced further by holding out one's hand unobtrusively and unmovingly, perhaps with a toy, so that the infant, if he or she wishes, can reach out and grasp it. Then, after you have proven yourself to be a safe person, the child may relax, probably will become curious, and may make the first move toward developing a friendly relationship. This is usually evidenced by the child trying to touch you, to grab your hand, or otherwise to attract your attention.

It is perhaps obvious by now that the main point in such an approach is simply to give the infant ample opportunity to look the helping professional over and to develop enough curiosity to make the first move. The most important thing about this approach is to avoid making any gestures that may be interpreted as being threatening by the young child. Such gestures, although it may be surprising to note, are not simply restricted to aggressive movements with your hands. For example facial contortions, particularly those friendly, broad smiles that are intended to amuse and to attract may have the opposite effect by frightening the young child and making him or her turn away. It is also not unusual, however, for very young children to be frightened simply by being stared at. The child may very well react as if staring were an aggressive activity or a threatening act. Moreover, even at the age of six or seven months, a child may be very sensitive to being stared at and will be much more comfortable if the therapist or counselor keeps his or her eyes averted or at least does not look the child directly in the eyes.

What about the anxious child? For one thing, it should go without saying that commonly it is best not to try actively to win over the anxious child's attention by means of grinning, clucking, or making funny faces. To a happy baby, such gestures may work very well; however, to a tense, anxious child, they can be very threatening.

On a related subject, the helping professional should expect different behavior from babies who are being raised in sterile institutions or otherwise who are deprived of maternal care. More specifically, these babies are frequently anxious and derive little pleasure from the things around them. It can also be expected that these babies' rate of psychosocial maturity is much slower than for others. Therefore, there should be no surpise to find such babies at the age of eighteen to twenty-four months behaving much like their more fortunate counterparts did at six months of age.

Returning to relatively normal development, the age of nine to approximately sixteen months is frequently referred to as the negativistic stage. That is the first attempts at socialization usually begin around this time and such result in a period of great frustration for the child. Therefore, these children often appear to be antagonistic at times, but usually quickly regain composure with a little acceptance and warm reassurance.

As will be discussed at the next chapter, babies usually do not begin to talk until reaching two or three years of age. In view of the fact that the infant discussed in this chapter cannot talk, attempting to communicate by talking is obviously limited. Nevertheless, just because the young baby cannot talk does not mean that talking on the part of the helping professional is totally meaningless or not worthwhile. Frequently, the very young child responds remarkably to the voice of the counselor or therapist, but not as much to the words as to the tone.

On the other hand, you should be cautioned that just because the child is too young to talk does not mean that he or she is too young to understand. More realistically, during growth and development, comprehension usually occurs a little before the ability to verbally express oneself. For this reason, the helping professional should never say anything in the presence of even preverbal children that he or she does not want the child to hear. Accordingly, an effort should be made to avoid saying anything that might be misinterpreted by the child.

MOTOR DEVELOPMENT

On a related subject, helping professionals should also be cognizant of the relatively normal advances of motor development, the most notable of which occur during the first fifteen to eighteen months of life. More specifically, most infants should be able to raise their heads unassisted by one to one and one-half months of age. Assuming further normal development, infants should be able to sit upright with support at around four to five months, sit upright without support at around six to eight months of age, stand or walk with assistance between nine to twelve months, and stand and walk without assistance between twelve and eighteen months of age. As previously mentioned, babies who are being raised in sterile institutions or otherwise who are deprived of maternal care may be expected to take more time in their motor development.

Of specific importance to the helping professional is to become generally familiar with the normal phases of motor development. This should assist the helping professional in utilizing observational skills in determining whether or not a particular infant should be referred for a psychological assessment. Moreover, such knowledge may serve as a reference for explaining to over-eager or anxious parents that their child appears to be developing well within normal expectations.

Chapter 3

CHILDREN AGE TWO TO ELEVEN

AGE TWO TO FOUR

SOMETIME around the age of two, most children begin to talk. For the child who can talk and has developed a beginning understanding of what is said to him or her, the situation markedly changes from the previous stage of development. However, in terms of successfully talking with a therapist, the change is not necessarily for the better until the child attains five to six years of age. Furthermore, children of this age have already become accustomed to being seen by physicians and nurses, and the therapist should avoid doing or wearing anything that might inadvertently lead the child to confuse the first session with him or her with previous visits to the pediatrician's office. For example the therapist should specifically avoid wearing lab coats and other similar clothing and not have anything in the office that might be interpreted by the child as being a potential instrument to being used for probing or puncturing.

One other specific example is clearly illustrated by the experience of a social worker who the author supervised a number of years ago. Namely, almost every time a young child entered her office, "screaming bloody murder" soon occurred. Following several discussions about this phenomenon, a visit to her office revealed that she had neatly placed a colorful "uncandle" on an end table, and a flowerpot her child had decorated with popsicle sticks sat on top of her desk. As the author surmised, the light blue "uncandle" reminded young children of an antiseptic canister containing forbidding instruments, and the popsicle sticks were equated with tongue depressors. Once these items were removed, no further significant problems were evidenced.

A further difficulty in communicating with children two to four years of age is that they tend to attach a peculiar, literal meaning to all words, including the words spoken by themselves as well as those spoken by others. Additionally, all actions, whether their own or those of others, are also regarded literally. Therefore, everything being direct and concrete, illustrations, analogies, and jokes have little or no meaning. Rather, everything is real, and they use a single-purpose, single-meaning approach to everything. Also, although they are capable of making certain deductions, they base them upon literal deductions rather than being able to generalize in the same manner as adults.

What all of this means to the therapist is that if he or she wants to get across to the child an accurate meaning, the selection of words must be chosen carefully and accurately with a conscious effort of avoiding the use of analogies. Furthermore when you have completed sending the specific message, you should check the result simply by asking the youngster to repeat back to you exactly what he or she heard you say. If this kind of precaution is not taken, you will have no idea of what peculiar notions or interpretations the child may have made in reference to what you intended to communicate.

This kind of literal approach that children take has been the butt of numerous jokes and cartoons. Many adults are delighted and amused in this two-plus-two-makes-four kind of cognition, and some parents are embarrassed as well as amused by it. Regardless, the therapist is well advised to avoid this type of reaction by attempting to view it as a natural part of human growth and development.

Obviously, examples of this are numerous. If a child

overhears his parent saying that Aunt Suzie is an old cow, the next time Aunt Suzie visits she may be asked to moo or to show how she makes milk. In essence, when a child overhears something said about an adult, he or she is very prone to make a literal interpretation of it. Unfortunately, this frequently results in the child being laughed at or rebuked.

With children three to four years of age, there can be no avoidance of this literal quality. Rather, it is a natural part of their development, but no matter how amusing, one which is best appreciated in silence, or at least not in their presence. For this reason, the helping person should take great care to avoid such seemingly harmless statements such as you are so cute I could eat you alive, or, you are so precious that I could just squeeze you to death. Remember, for the young child, this is literally what he or she may expect you to do.

Most unfortunately, no matter how devastating this can be, there appears to be no way to stop this kind of pain-inducing adult deception. In order to avoid this tragedy, the therapist is advised to be very literal or succinct and make himself or herself clearly understood. Furthermore, similes and complex comparisons should either be avoided or very carefully explained and clarified to the child.

An understanding of yet another quality of cognition, especially evident among two to four year old children, is important in communicating with them. This particular quality has to do with attributing life-like notions to inanimate objects, as though they were living things possessing a number of human attributes. More to the point, young children do not distinguish, as adults do, between what is alive and what is not. According to young children, tables and lamps and other household items possess the same feelings and cognitions that he or she does. For example it is not unusual for a young child two to four to say that a noisy vacuum cleaner is angry, but when it is turned off to say that it has gone to sleep.

For other reasons as well, the child of two to four can be very difficult to talk with. Namely, they tend to be overactive, hard to please or to satisfy, get into everything, and freely express all of their feelings. Also, nothing seems to have a lasting effect on them. For the social worker, this means that these children should not be expected to carry over any real understanding or acceptance of various explanations that may have been repeated again and again. Finally, the social worker will save himself or herself a great deal of disappointment by not expecting to be able to keep the attention of a three or four year old for very long. They are not being uncooperative but are simply behaving like three- or four-year-old children. For these reasons, the use of some form of play therapy can be very helpful. Accordingly, in addition to being a helpful diagnostic tool, games also tend to attract as well as hold the attention of children.

AGE FIVE TO SEVEN

Between the ages of five and seven, children are extraordinarily proud of their bodies and their possessions. Perhaps this is true of everyone to some extent; however, the situation is most acute at or around the age of five. Children of this age are extremely vain and consequently extremely afraid of any threat to their sense of perfection. In a directly proportional kind of way, the greater the value a child sets upon any asset, the greater will be his/her fear of losing it. For example, many a young boy has bragged about his muscles to his little sister, only to lose a fight with a little girl down the street the next day. To a youngster this age, such an experience can be expected to be devastating. He may take it so hard that you might think it was literally a matter of life or death.

The overreaction to loss of possessions is as true for girls as it is for boys. For example a little girl may be unrealistically devastated over misplacing a favorite pair of Aunt Janet's old high-heeled shoes. The important thing is not the shoes, but what the shoes represent. It is a personal possession, a part of herself. Its disappearance brings home to her the awareness or knowledge that life is not certain and that change and disaster can occur. An example from the author's own childhood was a torn and tattered old blanket that was treasured and protected as though it was life itself.

For these reasons, in probing for problems and concerns, the social worker is advised to avoid a direct or blunt approach. If you begin directly by saying, " I'm Mr. or Mrs. So-and-so, and I want to help find out what you and/or your family's problems are," all you can expect in terms of a reply is "There's nothing wrong with me." Such a response is not facetious, stubborn, or willful. The child must say there is nothing wrong with him or her, and he or she must deny complaints, in order to maintain his/her wish to be perfect, as well as to fend off any attack by the social worker, who after all, is interested in exposing what is wrong with him/her or his/her family. Of course, this is not really the goal of the therapist, but it is the initial perception of many young children.

What can be done about children hesitating to admit or to talk about problems and concerns? The thing for the therapist to do is to try as much as possible, to make it unnecessary for the child to feel so threatened or frightened. One might begin by asking questions to which the youngster can easily provide answers. For example you might determine any hobbies or sports the child is interested in, ask about them, and then gradually move on to what needs to be talked about. The important thing is to help the child to feel that he or she is safe enough and strong enough to continue to exist in spite of whatever problems the family may be experiencing.

Before proceeding to the next stage of development, two other subjects deserve attention. More specifically, somewhere around the age of four to seven, the development of a conscience, and a curiosity about sex or where babies come from begin to surface. Therefore, the therapist should be prepared for some rather blunt questions about sex, as well as a certain amount of guilt associated with the discussion of this subject. This matter is best approached by the therapist being prepared to provide factual information at a level that will satisfy the child's curiosity. Furthermore, one should not be surprised or shocked at the mistaken assumptions children frequently have about sex at this age. For example it is not unusual for little girls to express their anger at their mothers for having them born before growing a penis or for little boys to say that they are growing a baby in their belly. The social worker should also be prepared to offer appropriate assistance and information to the child's parents in a nonthreatening or demeaning manner.

AGE SEVEN TO ELEVEN

This age period is frequently referred to as middle childhood. It is characterized by increasingly expanding extrafamilial peer group and school related influences. It cannot be overemphasized that all children experience some psychosocial problems during this stage of development. However, if they are growing up in a healthy family environment, these problems are likely to be limited in their severity and a transient nature.

The birth order of children in this age group is helpful in understanding where the child is coming from in his or her communication with the therapist. For example the oldest child tends to be achievement oriented and to identify more readily with adults. Unfortunately, they also tend to be anxious and oversensitive. Hence, the therapist should avoid saying or doing anything that may be misinterpreted as being critical or threatening. Conversely, younger children are more open to accepting overt demonstrations of affection and tend to be more defiant and gregarious in their behavior. Furthermore, the middle child may be expected to be somewhat manipulative in dealing with the work around him/her.

Two other important considerations during this age period include sex role identification and continued development of a conscience. Namely, young girls are learning to respond to expectations of being neat, sociable, and inhibiting physically aggressive behavior, whereas boys are learning to be assertive, sometimes aggressive, ambitious, and above all, courageous. Finally, in terms of conscious development, these children are progressing from simple right or wrong notions to including the concept of equalitarianism. In communicating with children of this age group, the therapist should be particularly attuned to these two considerations, as well as to their frustrations over frequently being expected to act as an adult while being treated like a child. Therefore, acceptance and empathy are key ingredients or techniques in communicating with these children. Also, the therapist should studiously avoid expecting or pressuring these children to develop judgments about matters beyond their ability. They are still children and are more comfortable making decisions and forming judgments in things that are part of their world.

Chapter 4

SEPARATION FROM PARENTS, FEAR, AND CRYING

SEEING CHILDREN ALONE

S EEING young children other than in the presence of their parents frequently results in a very anxious and unhappy event. Moreover, the problem may be further exacerbated because very young children are unable or experience great difficulty in communicating clearly exactly what they fear.

The notion of separating a child from his or her parents usually brings to mind the picture of a child pitifully crying and yelling for his or her mother. However, this is not the only way young children attempt to cope with this kind of experience. It is not at all uncommon to find children who do not cry when their mothers or fathers leave the room. He or she may attempt to present a very stoic appearance and seem to be completely oblivious to the entire matter. Nevertheless, any careful observer will be able to readily identify the apparent signs of fear and anxiety on the part of very young children.

The author has observed a number of children who would cover their eyes and faces with their hands. Obviously, this is a magical way of attempting to cope with the situation, because the young child may literally believe that anything unpleasant that is out of sight is out of mind, and hopefully, ceases to exist. Other children may simply be too quiet, irritable, or become very figity. In any case, if the therapist is able to catch a glimpse of the child when he or she is unaware of being observed, that universally sad puppy dog look reveals exactly what the youngster is experiencing.

More specifically, separation almost always makes young children feel anxious and saddened. As we have seen though, very few, if any, very young children are able to express clearly or exactly what they fear. Therefore, what the social worker should remain cognizant of is that whether or not signs are clearly visible, feelings of fear and loss are probably present in all very young children who are separated from their parents.

What can the therapist do to help the child cope with the situation? One excellent approach is for the social worker to attempt to help children experience their unhappy feelings openly and honestly. This can be accomplished by knowingly and calmly saying to the child that you know that he or she must be a little afraid. At the same time, don't become alarmed if this initially results in the child crying even louder and harder. You might very well expect this kind of reaction for a time, but it should be percieved as being healthy and one that is usually of short duration.

Clearly, the child's greatest fear when parents leave the room is that they may not return. Unfortunately, words of reassurance do not always work the magic of producing a calm child, and the only way children can learn that their parents will return is through experience. It should be remembered, though, that even if a child has experienced the separation and return of his or her parents time and time again, the fear may be reawakened during stressful situations.

Being aware of this, the therapist can talk with their children about their fear and can assist them in expressing their fear through words. Thus, after helping the child express his or her fears adequately, the therapist can then offer reassurance that the parents certainly will return. Perhaps the most important thing to remember is not to reassure the child too soon. After all, you really should not expect children to believe you if you do not let them know that you understand how they feel. Furthermore, you may completely abort the opportunity of teaching the child how to constructively express and cope with fear if you offer reassurance too soon.

More specifically, children may have numerous reasons for fearing that Mom and Dad, when they leave them, may not return. Perhaps the most potent of these reasons is the fear that their parents no longer love them, and as a result, are happy to get rid of them. Accordingly, these children may believe that their parents no longer love them because they have been naughty or are inherently bad. Nevertheless, the more of the child's fears the therapist can help him or her to identify, the greater will be the possibility of the therapist being able to help the child to understand and overcome them.

This fear and similar ones may be so extreme as to render some children totally incapable of expressing them. Nevertheless, the therapist should attempt to express them for the child in an understanding manner, which may enable him or her to get in touch with them enough to be worthwhile. Thus, after having established the reality that the child is afraid his or her parents may not return, the therapist might say: "I get the impression that you're afraid your parents may not come back because they think you have done something bad and they are angry." If the child shows interest, the therapist might investigate further: "Perhaps you think your parents brought you to see me because you did something bad?" At this point, signs of further recognition by the child provides the therapist with an opportunity to begin drawing the child out by further enlarging on the subject. Finally, after the child has had an opportunity to ventilate all of his or her fears and doubts about the matter, the therapist can then safely explain that he or she is mistaken, that there is nothing bad about being here, and that his or her parents are not angry and certainly will return, just as they said they would.

Nonetheless, fear that their parents may not return is certainly not the only emotion children may experience when they are separated from their parents. It is not at all uncommon for young children to become angry when their parents leave the room. Some children may experience fear and anger simultaneously.

Moreover, children who respond with anger are usually distraught because their parents have deserted them and as a result, are making them suffer. Make no mistake, the anger is real, but sometimes it is so frightening that the child is unable to permit himself/herself to fully recognize it. Frequently, children will keep it hidden and express it only in disguised form or at special times. The author has observed a number of children who were cooperative and seemingly calm during their session with him, but who greeted their mothers or fathers in an ill-tempered manner. This angry behavior may also be directed toward anyone who takes his parents' place. Furthermore, psychoanalytic theory suggests that very young children may silently wonder why their parents have not returned. Are they ill, have they been injured, or are they dead? Of course, what lies behind all of this anxiety about their parents' welfare is a hostile wish to punish them for their most unjust behavior.

This unconscious wish to punish the offending parent may be expressed in a different way. The very sight of the returning parent may offer just enough reassurance for the youngster to feel safe enough to express some of his or her anger. Much to the chagrin of the parent, this anger may be expressed by totally ignoring their presence, as for the first, time playing with a toy and happily talking with the social worker. Usually though, this lasts only for a few moments, which is concluded by the child happily reaching out for their parent. Also, the child may begin to cry so profusely at this time as to give the impression that they are making up for the absence of tears during their meeting with the helping person.

This behavior is frequently confusing if not unsetting for parents. Namely, parents do not always perceive this teary reception as being a pleasant reunion. They may feel guilty or hurt by thinking that the child is not happy to see them. The helping person can offer helpful reassurance to parents by explaining that the child's anger or crying means that he or she is so happy to see them that it is only with their presence that he or she feels safe enough to express their feelings in an uncontrolled manner.

FEAR OF THE HELPING PROFESSIONAL

It is not unusual for very young children to be afraid of the professional during their first visit. As previously mentioned, the child may confuse a visit to see a helping person with previous trips to the pediatrician's office.

This particular fear can be further exacerbated by parents. Parents frequently threaten children with bogey men, doctors, and policemen if they don't promise to behave well. Although sometimes effective in frightening the unruly child into submission, it is an entirely improper method of influencing children to behave. Parents may also unwittingly encourage fear in the child through their own anxiety about what awful things the therapist might find out about them.

The therapist has an essential role to play in explaining to adult clients what may be expected during visits, but explaining this to very young children is difficult. Nonetheless, even though young children's understanding may be quite limited, it is never so limited as to justify a hopeless attitude. There is much to be gained by the professional discussing the general nature of visits with the child. Regardless of how little the child may appear not to understand or to listen, it is worthwhile to take the chance that something will be communicated.

CRYING

The crying of a very young child can be very heartbreaking, and the tears of the crying child during a session may be distressing to the professional. Such distress is not necessarily harmful, however greater degrees of distress on the part of the social worker can affect adversely one's effectiveness in relating to the child. Furthermore, heightened discomfort and anxiety may be perceived as being concrete evidence to justify the child's fear and continued sobbing.

Sometimes the therapist may feel so responsible for the child's unhappiness that he or she is overcome with guilt that he or she cannot concentrate. Actually, the therapist is not responsible for the child's crying anymore than he or she is responsible for the crying of an adult client, although adults cry for a different reason.

Children cry for the simple and direct reason that they are afraid or in pain. Usually, there is nothing subtle about it. What should be remembered though is that children are children, and the most that one can expect of them is that they behave in a way appropriate for their age. Furthermore, children are no different from most adults who can be expected to behave even less than their age when they are ill.

In conclusion, the therapist should not be upset by the crying of young children. Rather an effort should be made to demonstrate acceptance and understanding. The therapist would also do well to help the child put his/her fear into words. Conversely, the crying of young children is no indication for alarm, except when they fail to cry in appropriate circumstances or tend to express little or no affect.

Chapter 5

THE UNIQUE LANGUAGE OF CHILDREN

SYNCRATIC AND CRYPTIC LANGUAGE

IT should be emphasized at the outset that efforts to communicate with children frequently result in frustration and bewilderment. This should not be surprising, though, when one realizes that children, even at an age when it is possible for them to talk clearly, may appear to refuse to do so. This is often evidenced by the child talking irrelevantly and obscurely, consequently without comprehension. It is not uncommon for children to ask unrelated questions, give unrelated answers to the therapist's questions, or to simply go off on tangents of their own. Furthermore, it is also common for children to respond by asking a question in response to a question and not infrequently the child's question appears to come from out of the blue.

Child welfare and child development specialists have long known that children have a unique language peculiar to themselves. Moreover, because this syncratic language varies by age and is sometimes so individualized, it is not unusual even for their parents to experience difficulty in comprehending it.

With respect to age, very young children have only a limited number of words available to them and frequently resort to a form of sign language when their vocabulary fails them. For example very young children may have only a few words with which to express their anger, and as a result may physically strike out at an object or at someone in a

34

frustrated attempt to express this extreme emotion. It is also not uncommon for very young children to cope with such frustration simply by loud screaming.

However, considerably more subtle forms of communication may be used. For example a child may be harboring a great deal of hostility toward his or her parent, but refuse to acknowledge such when asked by the therapist. However the child may very well express his or her anger through playing family with dolls. More specifically, I have observed a number of children in this situation who would spank the "mommy" doll or offer very blunt and harsh reprimands to the parent figure. In this way, very young children are able to safely and sometimes quite vividly act out their anger, frustration, and passivity.

An important therapeutic goal of the therapist is to offer acceptance of the child's expression of extreme emotions and to help the child understand that temporary hostility and frustration are normal emotions that can be constructively managed. The therapist may also learn a great deal about what the child perceives as having prompted his/her feelings of discomfort. Moreover, it is also sometimes helpful to help children to express in words their feelings about the situation. This can be accomplished in a number of ways. For example after careful observation and demonstration of acceptance of the child's behavior, the therapist may simply attempt to put the child's feelings into words or offer to role play with him or her the situation that led up to the child's present emotional state. This approach offers the additional feature of not only helping children to learn to express their feelings, but also to practice different ways of resolving conflict.

Conversely, when children are older (between six and thirteen years of age), extreme emotions may not be so freely and vividly expressed in play. In this age range, youngsters are more likely to use words when expressing their emotions. Nevertheless, even though children of this age range may have developed considerable linguistic skills, they may still be expected to frequently express extreme emotions in a symbolic manner. This is, even though they may have a sufficient number of descriptive words in their vocabulary to fully express their feelings, they are prone to disguise in some manner that which they are really experiencing.

When thinking about the unique language of children between six and thirteen years of age, I am frequently reminded of several examples from my own experience. Namely, one seven-year-old girl asked me this seemingly serious question: "Where does rain come from?" However, when I proceeded to offer my best attempt at answering such a question, she responded with obvious indifference, and later indignantly shouted, "No, no, that's not what I mean!" Finally after regaining my own composure from such a seemingly demeaning reaction to what I thought to be an excellent response, I stumbled on to what the young girl really wanted to discuss. More specifically, I took time to examine the youngster's question from the perspective that it had a hidden meaning, was obviously important to her, but was something she did not feel comfortable addressing directly. So I said to her, "I suspect that your question 'Where does rain come from?' was really your way of asking 'Where do babies come from?'" A half-moon grin immediately appeared on her face, acknowledging that my interpretation was correct. We were then able to have a very constructive discussion of how babies are born, as well as an intense discussion of her feelings about the relatively recent arrival of her baby brother.

Another example: A ten-year-old boy asked this perplexing question: "Why do girl cows only give milk and bulls grow bigger and are killed for food?" My first impression was that the youngster was afraid of growing up and that this had something to do with sex. Fortunately, a little patience and further probing revealed that he only wanted to satisfy some of his curiosities about differences between the sexes.

I chose to include the second example for a very important reason. Namely, social workers, psychologists, and psychiatrists alike sometimes prematurely make their interpretations of what the clients say and do. More to the point, a little patience and further exploration frequently pays valuable dividends, especially when attempting to understand the unique way children sometimes communicate.

COGNITIVE CONSIDERATIONS

On another topic, very young children may be expected to communicate in another unusual way. Namely, it is not at all unusual for children two to three years of age to use one or two word sentences to convey messages. Every parent is familiar with the demanding one- and two-word chants of young children. Consider the following examples: "No!", "Me want!" "Now!" "Horsie!" and "Truck!" It never ceases to amaze me just how well these young children are able to communicate their wishes by using a few words.

Fortunately, as demanding as two- and three-year-olds can be, they are usually easily satisfied. This is most often accomplished as a function between fantasy and the emerging ability to accept a more readily available substitute for that which was originally desired. A good example of this is what very young children can and frequently do accomplish when given a simple pasteboard box in lieu of demands for a horse.

It should be clearly recognized that a tremendous increase in vocabulary occurs from about age two or three and on. Nevertheless, these children demonstrate little or no ability to understand and comprehend communication that requires reasoning at an abstract level.

Of particular significance for the therapist is that because young children's vocabulary outpaces their intellectual limits, it is easy to misunderstand them. More specifically, a child in this age range may very well use the word *justice* or *right*, but he or she may not mean exactly what adults think. More often than not, what children mean by such words is that something was fair or that some event should have turned out the way it did.

For true deductive reasoning to occur, children must attain ten to twelve years of age. Consider the following case example: Jimmy, an eight-year-old youngster, was advanced one grade and placed in a class for exceptional students. Much to the disappointment of his parents, he did exceptionally well in all of his subjects until introduced to very elementary concepts of physics. At this point, Jimmy became totally lost. Fortunately, as you may have guessed, Jimmy was indeed an exceptional student, and absolutely nothing was wrong with him. Rather, the problem was simply that the youngster had not yet matured to the point of being capable of performing the mental operations required for elementary physics.

Another frequently misunderstood thing about the unique communication of children is the difference of what is meant when they talk about sex differentiation prior to puberty and what they mean and understand about sex differentiation upon reaching puberty. More specifically, before reaching puberty, children mean and understand differentiation between the sexes, primarily based upon style of hair, dress, and perhaps even genitalia, but their concept includes nothing about sexual relationships.

In conclusion, it usually requires a good deal of study and direct practice experience to develop skill in understanding as well as fully appreciating the unique language of children. Nonetheless, the value resulting from the necessary time and investment required to understand children's unique way of communicating is realized through being able to understand not only what they are saying, but to develop sensitivity and appreciation for their real concerns.

Chapter 6

ADOLESCENTS AND TROUBLED TEENS

GENERAL CONSIDERATIONS

T HE problem of communication is compounded when clients reach puberty and adolescence. Certain general considerations include the fact that these youngsters have their own vocabulary, lack both physical and psychological stability, and experience frequent mood changes. Moreover, the vast majority of the problems are associated with sexual development, learning to relate to authority figures, and trying to develop their individual identities.

While I have known a number of therapists who attempted to keep up with the teenage vocabulary, I cannot recommend it. One reason is that any effort to do so would prove futile. A more important reason is that attempts to communicate with teenagers in their own language may give the impression that the therapist is being manipulative or condescending, which is usually disastrous. Alternatively, the helping person may lose the image of a professional helper and may appear to be a foolish adult trying to act young.

LACK OF STABILITY

As previously mentioned, one reason communication with teenagers is so difficult may be attributed to their normal lack of physical and psychological stability. More specifically, adolescence is characterized by change and instability. The adolescent is neither child or adult, nor is he

40

or she a combination. One of the more troublesome aspects of communicating with teenagers is that they are frequently part adult and part child and sometimes a little of both. Suddenly, a change occurs and everything becomes reversed.

One important consequence of this instability for the professional is to avoid getting caught in the trap of talking with adolescents as though they were only adult or only children. Namely, if the helping person decides to talk with adolescents as though they were only children, he or she runs the risk of insulting the part of the adolescent that is adult, and the reverse is true as well. Therefore, the therapist is caught in a seemingly impossible situation. Nonetheless, the solution rests squarely on the therapist's ability to develop an awareness and understanding of this important aspect of adolescence. More specifically, it is through such understanding and increased awareness that enables the therapist to effectively communicate, regardless of the instability during adolescence.

An illustrative example of the use of this understanding and awareness is revealed through the reaction of a thirteen-year-old boy I was seeing for the second time. Namely, in the middle of what appeared to be a low key discussion, I suddenly encountered a hurt reaction from him. I interpreted this as being a function of the instability during adolescence. My reaction was to clearly state that I had not intended to say anything that would hurt him and frankly admitted that I sometimes experienced difficulty in communicating with people his age and wondered if he might sometimes experience the same thing when talking with people my age. His response was simply a nod of agreement and a knowing grin on his face. In other instances, the professional might wish to be a little more direct in explaining what may be happening.

On a related subject, one should seldom if ever take

everything an adolescent says at face value. In spite of their claims of knowledge, awareness, and maturity, there is no such thing. Rather, adolescents simply try out certain aspects of maturity for size, so to speak, to determine what feels comfortable for them. Their claims for certain adult characteristics are also a way of compensating for the lack of these characteristics. Therefore, it is important for the helping person to be accepting of these normal characteristics of growing pains during adolescence, but to be fair and firm when circumstances require control. This is so, regardless of adolescents' demand for freedom and independence, as they also fear the possibility of going too far when appropriate limits are not established and enforced.

Other aspects related to instability may be summarized through variability in mood and moods of indifference. At one time, an adolescent may be enthusiastic and easy to communicate with. At another time, he or she may be antagonistic with little if anything positive to say. At other times, adolescents fall into a pattern of indifference with little or nothing to say except for a shrug of the shoulder and an occasional grin of embarrassment. This is an extremely difficult and anxiety producing experience for many therapists and other helping professionals as well.

These aspects of instability may best be understood and explained as functions of physical changes, psychosocial development, or both. With girls, the advent of breast development and menstruation can be exciting as well as frightening. To further complicate matters, these changes also produce and awaken certain confused but extremely potent feelings. Consequently, it is not unusual or incomprehensible for girls of this age to feel uncomfortable and experience difficulty in talking to a male professional. For this reason, I recommend that these clients be seen by a female or an experienced practitioner. A beginning male practitioner can overcome this difficulty as long as he is comfortable with his own sexuality and through the use of competent consultation and supervision.

On the other hand, male adolescents are also experiencing sexual development with consequent heightened and mixed feelings. More specifically, his beard is growing, his voice is changing, and he may be experiencing a spurt of growth and weight gain. Perhaps even more unsettling is the fear that he is not experiencing these changes as quickly as he thinks he should. Consequently, he may be very worried and preoccupied with fears of being different from his peers or afraid that he may never become a mature male. In summary, male sexual maturity is most obvious to him when he is able to achieve ejaculation. Concomitantly, his interest in the opposite sex is rapidly changing, as well as producing new problems for him.

The advent of masturbation is frequently a matter of concern for both both boys and girls, and sometimes for parents as well. Furthermore, it is not unusual for social workers, psychologists, psychiatrists, and other helping professionals to be asked to discuss masturbation with them. Therefore, the more you know and understand about the concerns and mistaken beliefs adolescents frequently have about this subject, the more effective you will likely be in responding the subject.

DISCUSSING MASTURBATION

Ordinarily, the best place to begin is to determine first what your client thinks about the subject, rather than to bluntly ask whether he or she masturbates, and if so, all of the other questions that may tend to follow. Their opinions about masturbation are likely to be considerably more revealing than detailed accounts of their own experiences. Frequently, these discussions of their general opinions are disguised accounts of their own activities and reveal their particular feelings, concerns, and false assumptions about masturbation.

The vast majority of fears and concerns surrounding masturbation are focused in some way on the possibility of physically and psychologically harming themselves. Not infrequently, these concerns include fears that masturbation may cause mental illness, brain damage, homosexuality, and the like. The most appropriate response to these concerns is to factually reassure the adolescent that there is no basis for their mistaken concerns.

Conversely, not all fears related to masturbation are concerned with the notion that the practice of it may be personally harmful. Namely, the most common fear among both boys and girls is the fear of losing control. Many feel that the act of masturbation is considered to be childish, a symptom of mental illness, or possibly an addictive behavior. Consequently, concerns about masturbation among both sexes frequently center around guilt, shame, and feeling inadequate and unable to control their sexual feelings and acts.

From another perspective, telling the adolescent that masturbation is neither wrong nor harmful is a matter of secondary importance. What he or she most urgently requires reassurance of is that there is no reason to fear that they are not normal or may have lost control of what they do. If the helping person understands this particular fear and concern and is able to help the adolescent to put his or her fears into words with specific respect to losing control, he or she will be of inestimable assistance.

What the therapist needs to understand is that both adolescent males and females feel a strong need to be in control of everything they do. Therefore, the helping person can help by saying that all young men and women worry about control, and many fear to some extent that the habit of masturbation is awful and hopeless because it cannot be stopped. Then, the adolescent should be reassured that control will come in time, and meanwhile nothing terrible will happen. It is also helpful to tell the adolescent that most people his or her age have similar problems and concerns.

It is not advisable for the practitioner to talk about his or her own fears and concerns about masturbation during adolescence. The reason for this is because upon hearing such, the adolescent may lose respect for the professional and may listen to nothing further that he or she has to say. More specifically, what the adolescent needs is not someone who may mistakenly be interpreted as being weak, but someone strong from whom he or she can derive support.

Two other fears more commonly expressed by boys are the fear of masturbating too much and consequently using up the amount of semen mystically allotted for his lifetime and fears of not masturbating enough. The latter fear is based upon the mistaken notion that semen continues to develop somewhere inside his body and failure to masturbate frequently enough may result in serious physical harm.

Returning to the matter of control, many boys are frightened by wet dreams. The fear is directly related to the fact that they occur involuntarily; this in turn implies a lack of control over their sexual behavior. As a result, it is not uncommon for many boys to masturbate frequently in hopes of preventing wet dreams.

On another matter, it is wise to very careful before volunteering advice about masturbation. The wise therapist will first request the adolescent to share what advice he or she may have already received, and from whom. It is also wise to avoid contradicting what the adolescent may have been told by respected people. Rather, it is better to simply reinterpret what the adolescent reported and interpreted having been told to him or her when he or she reports apparently false and damaging information.

TROUBLED TEENS

Recent years have witnessed an increasing concern about troubled teens in the United States, and in other countries as well. This has been evidenced by the increasing numbers of teenagers escaping from the pressures of growing up through alcohol and drug abuse, violent crime, and running away from home. Furthermore, I can attest to the validity of this concern based upon my own research and publication on the subject.

To be sure, the vast majority of these young men and women emerge from the normally troublesome teen years are fairly well-adjusted adults. Nevertheless, the lack of clear moral standards, consequent alienation, combined with pressure to become adults too fast are having a disastrous effect upon teenagers in America.

More specifically, too many parents either don't know how to communicate with their teenage children or are in such a hurry for them to assume adult roles and to achieve that they make their love and understanding contingent upon demonstration of these things. For these reasons, it is becoming more imperative for helping persons to become more skilled in communicating with adolescents, and just as important, to help more parents with the challenge of understanding and communicating with their children.

Chapter 7

COMMUNICATING WITH PARENTS

PARENTS AND PROBLEMS

ONE of the most salient features of working with children is the reality that work with children is difficult enough in and of itself, but in working with children, one must also work with parents. Working with parents is made easier when they are cooperative, when they know how to respond, and when the helping person is skilled in working with cooperative as well as uncooperative parents. Accordingly, attention to developing communication skills with parents is important, but so is giving attention to teaching parents how to better understand and more effectively communicate with their children.

In the first place, young children are able to provide little or no information toward developing a psychosocial history, and older children are limited in this respect as well. Therefore, parents are needed to provide information necessary for developing a psychosocial history of their child's birth, growth, and development. Also, with young children, parents play an instrumental role in the application of therapy, by modifying behavior in the home environment.

Fortunately, some parents are quite adept at providing this information, for example they have developed good observational skills and are factual as well as relevant in providing their descriptions. Nevertheless, a number of parents have little or no skills in observation or appreciation for providing factually relevant information and descriptions.

However, some parents tend to severely distort what they have observed, thus rendering what they offer either misleading or useless.

HELPFUL APPROACHES

Perhaps one of the best approaches is for the helping person to attempt to teach parents how to be more factual and descriptive. In so doing, the practitioner may provide an example of how he or she would present information about a child. Fortunately, most parents are able to learn a great deal about what is expected and needed by the helping person, when they are given a few examples.

Conversely, it is not entirely uncommon for some parents to be reluctant to offer very much information about their children. Their reluctance is frequently based upon the unrealistic fear that if they reveal something wrong or defective about their child, the practitioner may interpret this to mean that there is something seriously wrong with them as well. A helpful approach to this situation is to be honest and tell them that your purpose is not to find fault with them or their children. It is also helpful to explain to parents your objectives for each session or conference you have with them.

Unfortunately, there are times when parents are reluctant to provide necessary information or to be cooperative. The most salient of these circumstances is when the helping person is called upon to investigate the possibility of child abuse or neglect. Obviously, these parents are afraid of the possibility that their children will be removed from the home or of being charged with a criminal offense.

In these emotionally charged situations the therapist must keep clearly in mind his or her objectives as well as the purpose of child protection services. Of course, honesty is always the best policy, but the therapist will generate greater cooperation by demonstrating understanding, empathy, and concern for the parents as well. One approach is to tell the parents the purpose of the interview and to explain that you can imagine how unpleasant and uncomfortable they may feel, but you are also aware of just how many difficult and stressful situations parents are often confronted with. You may also wish to point out that regardless of what may or may not result from your investigation, you will be there to help. This is so, not only from the perspective of helping them to work toward the notion of preventing future problems, but also by helping them learn to deal with stress and develop better parenting skills, should their child be removed and they would like to work toward their child returning home.

Not infrequently, parents are so anxious as to appear unconcerned, uncooperative, and ignorant and have difficulty making any sense whatsoever. In these situations, the therapist can be helpful if he or she can enable the parents to recognize and discuss their fears and anxiety. More specifically, helping parents to get their fears out into the open greatly enhances the probability of their being able to be cooperative and helpful.

A closely related problem frequently stems from parents feeling that somehow they have contributed to their child's problem. This may reveal itself through parents wondering if the problem resulted from something they failed to do, insisting that there must be something more they can do, suggesting the use of other consultants, or by repeatedly asking the cause of the problem. Yet, many of these feelings and reactions are unconscious, and parents may have little or no awareness of their feeling of guilt. Moreover, it is this lack of awareness of their guilt feelings that causes them to behave as they do.

The therapist can be of assistance by recognizing any indications of guilt and by explaining to the parents that it is not at all uncommon for parents to feel responsible for their children's problems and difficulties. It is also helpful to reassure them that they were not to blame and that they are now doing something to help their child.

Accordingly, the therapist will do well to studiously avoid implying to parents that they were in any way the cause of their children's problem or difficulty. It is extremely unfortunate to find a number of therapists and helping professionals who unwittingly ask questions or make statements that give precisely that impression to parents. One way to check yourself for this particular problem is to tape and listen to yourself for a few sessions. Another approach for those with a strong constitution is to ask a colleague to listen to the session with you and provide constructive feedback.

AVOID BECOMING ANGRY

A common problem for beginning therapists is to be tempted to believe that certain parents are bad for their children. Obviously, this is frequently true, but one should also be careful to look for positive influences parents have on their children as well. Unfortunately, far too many students graduate with the impression that their primary professional responsibility is to look for weaknesses in their clients. Therefore, it should be pointed out that one can only build upon strengths, which is particularly true when talking with parents.

Another frequent occurrence when talking with parents is to be cognizant of the fact that many parents will repeat to their children what the therapist has discussed with them. Certainly, it is wise to request parents not to repeat certain things to their children, but even this is not a guaranteed safeguard.

More specifically, most practitioners do occasionally become frustrated or angry with at least some parents. When this occurs, it is often helpful if the helping person takes time out to review the situation. Frequently, the source may be certain traits or characteristics that remind the helping person of unpleasant memories of their own parents. On the other hand, the frustration may derive from parents continually distorting or simply failing to follow through with suggestions offered by the helping person. The former is usually readily resolved after discussing it with a supervisor or respected colleague. The latter, if it persists, should alert the helping person to look for a possible mental deficiency, or for a serious emotional problem on the part of the parent. This is particularly evident with parents who once provided appropriate nurture and care for their children, but who abruptly become neglectful or abusive.

STEPPARENTS AND STEPFAMILIES

Unfortunately, even though statistics reveal an ever increasing number of stepfamilies in this society, a paucity of published research is available on the subject. More specifically, very little is known about the stepfamilies' complexities and significant factors, which should be understood by therapists and other helping professionals.

Nonetheless, I will propose a few suggestions based upon my own experience and research that may be useful. First, one should consider whether the previous marriage or marriages were terminated by divorce or death of a spouse. It usually takes a little more time for people to make the necessary adjustments to divorce than is ordinarily required in dealing with the death of a spouse. This is particularly so when the parent you are working with did not want the divorce. It is not uncommon to find parents whose previous marriage was terminated by the death of a spouse to engage in idealizing the deceased for quite some time. Second, be prepared for a variety of patterns among remarried parents in terms of how they compensate or overcompensate through their children, as well as through various demands and expectations made on their new spouse. Third, but certainly not least, be prepared to help children reintegrate into the new family structure and do not be surprised to find parents who are originally awarded custody to suddenly desire to shift all parental responsibility back to the other spouse. This is particularly prevalent not long after remarriage. The most important tasks of the helping person are to familiarize himself or herself with the growing literature on stepfamilies, and to become able to differentiate between assumptions and problems applicable to intact nuclear families and those applicable to stepfamilies' life-style.

SINGLE PARENTS

Single-parent families do not differ a great deal from stepfamilies. Nonetheless, a few generalizations about certain differences may be helpful in better understanding these parents.

More specifically, based upon my research and experience, single parents frequently experience financial problems, based on a sudden reduction of income. Moreover, single-parent fathers frequently report problems with learning general housekeeping skills and financial problems related to babysitting expenses and the cost of eating out rather than preparing most meals at home. Finally, a number of single-parent fathers and mothers report an increase in alcohol consumption, a general frustration, mild depression, as well as anger and loneliness. Nonetheless, perhaps the most important implication for the helping person is to remain alert for the possibility of single parents inappropriately venting their anger and frustration toward their children. The helping person would also do well to consider these parents' potential for role overload in the sense of playing the role of mother, father, and in many cases, boyfriend or girlfriend. It is also important to pay particular attention to parents who suddenly lose a spouse through death as they frequently experience severe financial and emotional problems.

POSITIVE REGARD FOR PARENTS

A good deal has been written about positive regard, and perhaps no other factor is as important when communicating with parents. Namely, a primary distinguishing feature between the helping person who communicates easily with parents and one who does not is revealed in the way he or she regards parents.

The successful helping person tends to regard parents as being assets and as being extensions of himself or herself in the treatment process. In other words, parents are without question an indispensable aid to the helping person. Conversely, the practitioner who has problems working with parents sometimes regards them as being unable to help and ignorant and as an interference that would be nice to avoid.

Accordingly, parents do present their own complications, but there is no way of denying the reality that successful work with children is to a great extent dependent upon them. The helping person who recognizes this will be better equipped to put himself or herself in their position and will have a better understanding of how to capitalize on what they have to offer, and in the end, the child will be the benefactor.

SECTION II

ADULTS AND THE AGED

Chapter 8

HOSTILE AND OVERLY
AFFECTIONATE CLIENTS

COMMON PROBLEMS

UNFORTUNATELY, a very common as well as frequent problem is to be presented with a client who is
suspicious or overtly antagonistic. Given such a situation,
many therapists are prone to meet hostility with hostility, or
attempt to ignore it, gloss it over, or to directly tell the client
that he or she should not be suspicious or angry. It may be
effective for some therapists to express anger toward an
angry client, but a far more constructive approach is to
make an effort to find out what is behind the client's anger.
Whatever you do, try not to simply gloss it over or to ignore
it. Instead, it is better to meet it openly, if possible, calmly,
and in that way help the client to talk about his or her angry
feelings.

Ordinarily, when a client is hostile toward his or her
helping person the source of the anger exists somewhere
within the client. This is particularly so when the therapist is
seeing the client for the first time. Nonetheless, it is possible
for the therapist to do or fail to do something that elicits
anger from a client. Therefore, the therapist should not be
completely absolved of all responsibility if a client should
become hostile toward him or her. Fortunately, though, in
most cases the therapist is guiltless and simply represents
someone toward whom the client is able to express his or her
hostility.

One of the most frequent mistakes beginning therapists

tend to make is to assume responsibility for the client's state of anger. Nothing could be further from the truth. Anger is a universal emotion the therapist should accept and be able to permit his or her client to express.

Certainly, there is no reason to permit clients to become physically aggressive toward you. Nonetheless, there are a number of benefits that may be accrued by permitting as well as encouraging clients to verbally express their anger. One specific benefit is to provide your client with the opportunity to learn to constructively express anger. Other benefits include the possibility of learning certain things about your client that he or she is unable to express otherwise; helping your client to develop useful problem solving skills; and finally, permitting your client to verbally express anger without rebuke frequently results in the development of a relationship based upon trust and confidence between the client and therapist.

WHEN CLIENTS MAKE YOU ANGRY

One thing I can tell you for certain is that one day you will meet a client whom you dislike. This dislike is usually based upon some kind of prejudice and/or a strongly opposed value. Nonetheless, whatever the source, it can lead to serious difficulty in communicating with your client.

Now, most of my students are quick to disclaim any prejudice and admonish me for even suggesting that they will eventually meet a client whom they will dislike. Accordingly, this is exactly the way they feel and what they believe until I ask them how they feel about people who knowingly discriminate against the less fortunate and more poignantly, their feelings about parents who physically and sexually abuse their young children. At this point, my students begin to recognize that anyone who has a value system, and certainly everyone does, cannot help being prejudiced to some degree, or more specifically, to hold values that are opposing to certain values held by others.

Most assuredly, no therapist should be asked to completely abdicate his or her values regarding moral as well as social issues. So too, no therapist should be expected to not take a stand on anything. To do so would rob the therapist of any opportunity to advocate on behalf of his or her clients.

Nevertheless, when it comes to doing your job, you must be able to free yourself in a way that makes possible unlimited treatment of the client, regardless of what he or she may represent. One solution of course is to turn the client over to another therapist and in some instances this may well be the most constructive thing to do.

More to the point, other than referral, what can you do when you find yourself in a position where you dislike or are angry with a particular client? The first step is to get in touch with what you are telling yourself about the client. Accordingly, to my friends Doctor Albert Ellis and Doctor Maxie Maultsby, who are the founders of rational emotive and rational behavior therapy respectively, most undesirable feelings or emotions are derived from irrational things we tell ourselves about people, or more specifically, activating events. By irrational, they mean thoughts or statements we make to ourselves and accept as truths or as a part of our belief system, without having tested them against objective reality.

I am reminded of a staff member who came to my office one day and exclaimed, "I don't like the client I just saw and I would like for you to assign him to someone else." A little gentle probing revealed that what the social worker found to be annoying was the fact that his new client frequently interrupted him in middle of a sentence. What the young man was telling himself about his client or activating event was that the client was unlikeable because he didn't respect him, had no appreciation for his professional training, and so on, but that he should do or have all of these things. My question was simply to ask, "Why should he?" Needless to say, the social worker was unable to provide any verifiable or objective basis for clinging to the belief that his client should possess any of the alleged qualities. As a result, the social worker's extreme dislike for his client soon dissipated.

For the most part, a good deal of anger or dislike toward clients can be handled through rational self-analysis. However, there are also times the therapist experiences feelings of dislike or anger toward a client but is unable to identify any apparent reason for such. It is also not uncommon for the helping person in this situation to experience a guilty reaction. Here too, rational self-analysis for the basis of the guilt reaction is effective, but it is also helpful to recognize that these clients may very well represent other persons toward whom the practitioner has felt angry. Accordingly, it is best not to try to force yourself to like these clients, as this would be impossible. Nevertheless, it is advisable to practice rational self-analysis as well as to discuss the situation with a respected colleague or supervisor.

MASKED HOSTILITY

What about the client who is experiencing anger but is unaware and unable to express it? For one thing, manifest or open anger may sometimes be uncomfortable for the therapist, but it is certainly easier to handle. Nonetheless, when a therapist senses something that suggests anger or hostility in a client, an effort to help the client get in touch with and to express his hostility is helpful.

More often than not, masked or hidden hostility is very

deep-seated. Also, any strong emotion if left unexpressed cannot only seriously interfere with the relationship between the therapist and the client but may be devastating for any efforts at treatment.

Sometimes it is very helpful and effective for the therapist to state directly to the client that perhaps he or she is angry. On the other hand, this direct approach sometimes is responded to by silence and a fearful expression on the client's face. The reason for this is because many people have come to believe that any admission, much less expression of anger, is closely akin to an unpardonable sin. For these clients, it is more helpful to approach the issue somewhat less directly, by using less threatening words.

I recollect one client who was obviously hostile, but was not expressing it, to whom I suggested that she must be angry. Her response was dead silence and an obvious facial expression of fear. Fortunately, I recognized what was happening, retreated, and clarified that she must be unhappy about whatever it was that we were talking about at the time. This served to effectively break the barrier for her and she was eventually able to get in touch with and to express her hostility. Finally, it is also very important for the helping person to respond to the client's expression of masked or hidden hostility with acceptance and genuine positive regard.

OVERLY AFFECTIONATE CLIENTS

Everyone wants to be liked, and helping professionals are no exception. It should also be recognized that helping professionals tend to enjoy and to be more effective with clients who like and respect them. However, respect and feelings of admiration should never be confused with romantic or blatant sexual attachments, which may develop suddenly, without warning, and for no apparent reason. This type of affection on the part of a client can be and frequently is more upsetting to helping professionals than is open hostility.

I am reminded of a particular psychiatrist who encountered just such an overly affectionate client. Unfortunately for him and his family, the court ruled that he responded to the situation in less than a professional manner. The end result was the permanent loss of his license to practice psychiatry. How much of what actually happened was factual, contrived, or otherwise cannot be said for certain. Nonetheless, his particular experience should serve to remind other helping professionals of the serious implications of dealing with overly affectionate clients.

Another example derives from my own experience as a student, when I was much less experienced. Namely a female client three to five years my senior began to be very complimentary and suddenly one day asked if I would have dinner with her at her house. In somewhat of a state of panic, I prematurely rushed in and explained that this was not possible or appropriate because of our professional relationship. Much to my chagrin, the next day she phoned me to explain that we could now have dinner at her apartment because she had hired another therapist.

Frequently, when a client blurts out something suggesting affection or sexual overtures, the helping professional is caught off guard and is at a loss as to what to do. Sometimes one is tempted to take personal affront and to rather indignantly point out to the client that his or her behavior is inappropriate. On other occasions, the helping professional may be tempted to dismiss the matter by joking about it. In any case, many professionals would like to quickly dismiss it in some manner and go on to some other more agreeable or comfortable matter.

Nevertheless, helping professionals should avoid falling in the trap of being too quick to dismiss statements of affection by their clients. Rather, it is more helpful and frequently more productive to try to look behind what they appear to be saying. For example such statements frequently represent a desperate plea for approval or are indicative of other problems. On other occasions, overly affectionate or complimentary statements on the part of clients may be a way of attempting to reassure themselves that the helping professional is competent and understanding enough to clearly warrant sharing painful and highly emotional experiences. Then again, some compliments are quite genuine and well intended. In such cases, the helping professional may be very justified in stating his or her appreciation and experiencing good feelings about oneself. However, in a manner of speaking, he or she should not be too hasty to dismiss it or to partake of too much of the pie. Such behavior can be devastating to the client as well as for the helping professional.

Helping professionals who deal with patients on a physical basis, for example physicians and nurses, frequently encounter patients who develop emotional attachments. In these instances, it is most often a kind of self-reassurance that he or she is doing the appropriate thing by trusting the physician or nurse. This usually occurs right after surgery or the discussion of a previously hidden but painful experience. However, if the particular helping professional is able to calmly accept and understand their meaning, the patient's affectionate state usually soon dissipates back to a more rational and appropriate level.

At other times, some clients behave in open and blatantly seductive ways. In such cases, the helping professional must learn to realize and understand that such feelings derive from within their clients or their personal situation, but in no way evidences attractiveness on the part of the helping professional. These kinds of pseudo attachments may also be a function of the helping professional's position, title, or father or mother image. Obviously, it would be extremely unethical for any helping professional to even consider the possibility of taking advantage of this kind of sexual displacement.

Unfortunately, when a helping professional becomes aware that he or she is the object of sexual attraction on the part of a client, it had usually progressed beyond the point of avoiding a certain amount of unpleasantness. For this reason, it is far more preferable to learn to recognize the early signs of this kind of development and to deal with it as early as possible.

In conclusion, if a client does declare affection or makes advances, the helping professional is pressed to say something about the situation. Rather than to ignore or joke about it or ring for a colleague, one is much better off to seriously say something like this, "I can see that your feelings are aroused or attached to me, but this is because of the help you sought and the trust in our relationship. It is certainly not an unusual phenomenon and is quite understandable, but is something that I cannot be a party to. In other words, you are here for the purpose of seeking help, and I am here to provide the very best professional services possible." In many instances, this resolves the matter, but in others, clients may either become angry or persist. Finally, this exchange should be recorded in the client's chart as a matter of factual record should the matter develop completely beyond proper perspective.

Chapter 9

MENTALLY DEFICIENT CLIENTS

INTRODUCTION

THE level of a client's intellectual defect is ordinarily described as being mild, moderate, severe, or profound. While psychological tests and their scores are important in determining the level of deficiency, other factors are usually relied upon as well. The most important of these other factors is the person's social adjustment.

Communication with retarded clients always presents certain problems as well as difficulties. Perhaps the first and most significant of these problems and difficulties is directly related to the problem of identifying and diagnosing the presence of subnormal intelligence in a client. Certainly, gross or severe mental deficiency is a relatively easy circumstance for even beginning helping professionals to recognize. However, there are those clients who function at higher levels, not too far below the average range of intellectual functioning, who may for all facts and purposes appear to be perfectly normal, exhibiting little indication of mental deficiency. Nevertheless, the client's behavior and vocabulary are the most revealing indices for the therapist to rely upon in assessing intellectual capacity.

BEHAVIOR

As a general rule of thumb, the therapist can safely assume that the lower the intelligence, the less complicated the behavior a client will be able to demonstrate or to carry out. With adults, the easiest form of behavior to elicit and determine is the client's job and associated skills required for satisfactory performance. The best way to approach this is to find out what the client does for a living and to discuss the kinds of things he or she does while working. The ordinary data contained in a psychosocial history may not be very informative in this particular respect. More often than not, it will probably state that the client works in a certain business and his or her income is at a particular level. Unfortunately, unless the helping professional takes the time to explore the matter further, he or she may never discover that the client sweeps the floor and delivers messages.

More specifically, the mentally deficient client is most likely to have a relatively simple job that requires few cognitive skills as well as very little if any responsibility. Furthermore, the job is usually repetitious and one that most people would not aspire to have.

Ordinarily, the helping professional will not approach the subject of a client's occupation unless he or she has reason to suspect some form of mental deficiency. However, when the therapist begins to notice repeated deficiencies in the client's behavior, he or she would be well advised to suspect and to investigate the possibility of mental deficiency. Finally, some of the more common of these behaviors include the client's failure to carry out simple instructions, the inability to describe their problem, and other peculiar or seemingly uncooperative behavior. Of course, this kind of behavior can also be indicative of certain mental illnesses as well.

VOCABULARY

Another extremely helpful way to roughly assess a client's intelligence is to pay very careful attention to the words clients use to express themselves. Moreover, the most sensitive parts of tests that have been designed to measure intelligence are based upon the person's vocabulary. That is, the more intelligent he or she is, the larger the number of words he or she will use correctly. Conversely, the fewer the number of words correctly used by clients, the lower will be their intelligence.

Accordingly, the helping professional should not be misled by a client's poor grammar, English, or choice of words. This kind of talk on the part of clients does not necessarily suggest mental deficiency, but may be more a function of education and environment.

Nonetheless, if the helping professional, while talking with the client, observes a greater than usual limitation in the selection and use of words, he or she should suspect that the client is functioning at less than average intelligence. The therapist can further verify this observation simply by consciously using increasingly difficult words and observing the client's response to determine if he or she understands them.

ARITHMETICAL SKILLS

The client's ability to correctly manipulate figures can also reveal a great deal about his or her intellectual capacity. However, even though this varies closely with the level of intelligence, it is not always as reliable as is their vocabulary. This is primarily so because some people have an unrealistic or neurotic fear of numbers and their manipulation. Nevertheless, if a client demonstrates reasonable ability with figures, serious mental deficiency can be ruled out.

SPECIAL PRECAUTIONS

The significance of having some awareness that a client

is mentally deficient, is because if it is not recognized and taken into account, it can mean the difference between success and failure. More specifically, mentally deficient clients require talking to and care very different than that required by clients of normal intellectual capacity. Simpler words greatly enhance communication, as does the avoidance of complicated instructions. Closer supervision should also be maintained.

The importance of close supervision cannot be overemphasized. With some clients, it may be advisable to enlist the aid of a relative, friend, or neighbor. This is important to ensure that what the helping professional wants to have carried out is accomplished in a reasonable manner.

PARENTS

Telling parents that their child is mentally deficient can be a very difficult and highly emotional task for some helping professionals. It is also a very emotional and traumatic experience for the parents as well.

The initial reaction of parents is usually a mixture of shock and denial. This should not be surprising though, for no parent wants their child to have to experience any kind of problem, especially a mental deficiency.

Nevertheless, the most difficult thing for the helping professional to help parents with is their extreme feelings of guilt. This also frequently results in each investigating their own and their spouse's family history for occurrences of mental deficiency. What unfortunately but frequently ensues after each completes their investigation is blame, heightened guilt, and a breakdown in marriage and family relations. Consequently, the most unfortunate result of all of this is that just when family members are in need of support from each other, they are least capable of giving it.

The helping professional must intervene on an intensive basis when marriage and family relations begin to deteriorate. Parents must be provided with factual information and advised accordingly with respect to the care and management of the mentally deficient child.

Fortunately, a great deal more is available for assisting the mentally deficient and their parents than what was available only a few years ago. So too, new knowledge has been discovered as well as more effective techniques and programs for training, care, and management.

When communicating with parents of a child who has a mental deficiency, the helping professional must be aware and remain sensitive to the dynamics involved. In essence, one needs to be strong enough to control the situation by confronting the parents with reality, yet sensitive enough to be supportive and helpful. For example it is sometimes necessary to sit the parents down and firmly tell them that whatever the cause may be, nothing can be done about that now. However, certain decisions and actions can be made at this time that can affect you and your child from this point on. Sometimes, it is also helpful to add that the child is a product of both parents, that he or she can be a special joy within his or her own limits, and that you are there to help them realize this to the maximum possible limit. Nonetheless, the helping professional should, at all costs, avoid becoming personally involved and offering unrealistic hope.

Chapter 10

CHRONICALLY ILL AND HANDICAPPED CLIENTS

INTRODUCTION

CARING for the chronically ill patient requires effective communication skills of all of the helping professionals. These skills extend as well into communication and respect of the knowledge of each team member. Continuity of care is an important aspect in this situation, for the majority of patients require hospitalization at intervals. The goal of the clinically based helping professional is to aid the patient in returning to the community in a functional and meaningful capacity. If the helping professional's primary practice is not located in the clinical or hospital setting, a basic knowledge of the disease process and its limitations should be obtained. This, in combination with an accurate social history, can tell a great deal about the emotional trauma the patient is going through in his or her adaptation to the disease process.

Care must also be taken in respect to family members and their reaction to the illness. A fear of burden may lead to ambivalent feelings regarding hopes of recovery. Guilt and depression may quickly follow these ambivalent feelings toward a loved one.

Chronic disease processes may take varying forms. Debilitation may be rapid, as in the case of the complete stroke patient, with rehabilitation slow, or the debilitation may be slow with periodic lapses in progression. Causative factors of the disease process may vary, some being congenital in nature, and others enhanced by life-style. Both of these areas should be taken into consideration by the helping professional, regardless of his or her area of expertise, and steps toward basic self-education should be undertaken.

There are many disease processes that will be seen by the helping professional. However, only a few generalized states frequently seen in our population and a few that drastically alter life-style will be discussed. As previously mentioned, the majority of patients with chronic disease processes will most probably be hospitalized at some point. Perhaps it would be appropriate to briefly mention communication with the hospitalized patient who is unable to communicate himself or herself. The examples that come to mind are intensive care patients, perhaps a severe asthmatic on a respirator and unable, consequently, to talk, or the recent stroke victim who appears comatose and has not yet begun to regain function. It must be remembered that although these patients are unable to communicate verbally, and perhaps not even nonverbally, the sense of hearing remains the most acute. Reassurance is imperative at this point in the patient's recovery, for one can imagine the fear and anxiety being experienced. Although no apparent response to communication is forthcoming, these patients do hear and many times are able to reason and understand, as well as remember. Their only means of understanding and reassurance is through the communication of the health professional.

STROKE

One of the devastating things that can physically happen to an individual is a stroke. An active and alert person in a matter of moments, suddenly becomes helpless and dependent. An important point to remember is that this also changes the lives of each family member, and as was pointed out earlier, may cause some ambivalent feelings on their part. Patients experience the fear of incapacity for life and of losing their minds, as well as the fear of death. Much progress has been made in the area of physical therapy for these patients, and many return to lead meaningful and productive lives in the community. The onset of illness is very rapid, and progress, as a rule, is slow. All of these things should be taken into consideration when dealing with these particular patients, as well as their families.

Helping professionals who work with stroke patients, especially in the acute phase of recovery, often become exasperated in their inability to do anything definitive quickly for these patients. The helping professional must watch for this quality in himself or herself so that he does not become indifferent, and worse yet, antagonistic toward the patient and his family because of his or her own frustrations. This situation can also be encountered in the office setting, for these patients may make inappropriate movements, or at times, not respond when spoken to. One must remember to be aware of sensory deficiencies of the patient and to cater to them. One example is to approach the patient with impaired vision from his unimpaired side.

Dealing with stroke patients and their families is a frustrating task for the helping professional, the patient, and the family alike. Although progress is painfully slow and adaptation to the sudden physical impairment is difficult, dealing with these patients can indeed be rewarding.

RENAL FAILURE

When one thinks of kidney failure, hemodialysis (or the *kidney machine*) immediately comes to mind. This breakthrough in modern medicine has enabled many to lead longer and more comfortable lives. These patients undergo many emotional changes in coping with and adapting to their new life-style, and as a rule, social service as well as psychological services are enlisted.

Renal failure may occur from several different sources and may either be slow or fast in onset. If there is no chance of renal function returning, however, the patient must face the reality of marriage to the kidney machine for the rest of his or her life. Reactive emotional depression is frequently seen in these patients especially during the acute phase of recovery.

The kidney obviously filters the blood of the body's waste products. In the nonfunctioning kidney, these wastes remain in the blood causing azotemia and uremia with resulting mental confusion if allowed to continue. Hemodialysis closely mimics the action of the kidney and may be done two or three times a week on an outpatient basis. However, this is based upon the patient's particular needs. The procedure is time-consuming and not entirely painless. Several methods are utilized, but the basic is access to both a vein and an artery of the patient. This can be done through the use of needles or through the insertion of a shunt connecting the two. The shunt protrudes from the skin to enable easy access; so altered body image and consequent emotions must be dealt with.

In order for dialysis to be successful, full patient cooperation is required, and much teaching as well as reassurance is required. This particular patient has much to deal with and is active in his or her medical care. Discussion of a few of the problems the renal failure patient must cope with may be helpful at this point.

Patients are provided with special clamps to be carried with them at all times because the shunt may inadvertently become disconnected. In that particular case, massive hemorrhage would occur from the arterial site, and death would ensue unless the shunt is immediately clamped. The patient lives with this possibility, although rare, every day. The shunt must be watched closely and to make certain that it remains patent, or open. With patients who undergo dialysis for an extended period of time, the necessity to reinsert several shunts is not uncommon. As a rule, general anesthesia is not utilized, because of the degree of illness of these patients, so again the procedure is not the most comfortable, although local anesthesia is utilized with sedation. This may serve to explain some of the heightened anxiety prior to surgery.

To decrease the frequency of dialysis, the patient is put on a very strict diet of restrictions concerning protein, sodium, potassium, and fluid intake. These restrictions are severe and may result in greatly cramping the life-style of the patient.

Renal failure patients frequently have chronic anemia, which tends to decrease their energy level. They are also highly susceptible to fractures as well as infections. If the helping professional has a cold, for example, he or she must be sure to alert this particular patient of his condition and perhaps postpone his or her appointment. Discussions with these patients should be brief so as to avoid tiring them.

All of this is mentioned to alert the helping professional not to treat lightly the degree of despair experienced by many of these patients. The helping professional may feel that the patient should feel lucky to have a machine available that can keep him alive and to be able to live at home and to function in the community. The restrictions on life are numerous, and the constant fear of pain and death is realistic as well as ever present.

Another area that should be considered with the kidney patient is the possibility of organ transplant. The stress of being "on the list" for tissue match at kidney salvage centers is great. Live donors in the patient's immediate family are also a source of transplant, in which case both patients may need emotional support.

Recovery from a kidney transplant is a stressful time. The patient feels well, but strict isolation procedures are undertaken to avoid all possible risk of infection. This can be a lonely time for the patient, for the idea of body rejection is constant.

CONDITIONS OF ALTERED BODY IMAGE

The convalescence of a burn patient is a long and tedious one. Initial treatment of the patient requires much reassurance on the part of the helping professional. Depending on the extent and location of the burns, altered body image could be severe. If the burns are severe and extensive enough, repeated surgery is required, including debridement of the area as well as skin grafting. Both procedures are quite painful, and isolation is required to decrease the chance of infection. What is commonly referred to as the *intensive care syndrome* is commonly seen in these patients, including withdrawal, depression, and regression. After the patient has survived the horrifying ordeal of the accident and returns to the community, intensive social services and psychological counseling is generally required. Scarring from burns is not a pleasant sight. Although much progress has been made in skin grafting and plastic surgery, the results do not approach that which nature gave us. Also, before reconstructive or cosmetic surgery is undertaken, the original wounds must be completely healed, and this could take months.

Amputation of a limb is a sad occurrence, especially when it involves the very young. A traumatic injury, as in automobile or motorcycle accidents, is the most frequent cause for need of amputation in our youth, and it can involve a great deal of guilt as a part of the mourning process. Great strides have been made in vascular repair, which could save the limb. In some cases, though, this seems to simply prolong the inevitable and deepen the depression. Altered body image is important in these cases. The stump must be completely healed before a prosthesis can begin to be used; so mobility may be decreased for some time. It also takes a great deal of work and determination on the part of the amputee to learn to use the prosthesis, and a good deal of support and encouragement is helpful.

Arthritis is a crippling disease seen in all age groups of our population. It is generally a slowly progressive disease that requires a good deal of adaptation in life-style. At this point patients are in need of reinforcement and encouragement to keep moving to decrease the crippling effects. The helping professional should also keep in mind the need for these patients to stay independent as long as possible. The office area should have chairs that will be easy to get in and out of. Extremes of temperature affect the stiffness these patients experience after periods of inactivity. This should be kept in mind in the placement of furniture, with particular respect to air conditioning vents.

PULMONARY DISEASE

There are several classifications of pulmonary diseases, some that are congenital in origin, others infectious, and those that are enhanced by life-style. The latter category is selected for discussion at this point.

Lung cancer comes to mind first in the life-style-enhanced pulmonary diseases. Although different causes also play a part, every smoker is well informed as to the possible outcome of his or her habit. Therefore, guilt and remorse must be dealt with in these patients. The fear of reoccurrence is a real concern.

Treatment of the families of the "chronic lunger" or patient with emphysema is very intense. Exemplary of this situation was a professional colleague who watched her father slowly die of emphysema over a period of years. In the latter stages, he was unable to breathe without supplementary oxygen, and he wheeled his oxygen tank with him everywhere. Every breath was a gasp. It should be obvious by now that families suffer along with their loved ones, but they also have ambivalent feelings analogous to those of the stroke victim's families.

OTHER CHRONIC MEDICAL ILLNESSES

There are many other medical illnesses that can be well controlled medically but that only a few years ago were usually terminal. Change in life-style in the majority of these disease processes is moderate in comparison to those previously mentioned. Any need to facilitate a change in life-style is emotionally trying. It also brings to reality one's own vulnerability, diminishing youth, and ultimate death.

Diabetes is seen in our population in the very young, as juvenile onset diabetes, and among the aging, as adult onset diabetes. Diabetes melitus can be very devastating disease, especially the juvenile-onset type. Some of the consequences include blindness and difficulty in healing simple wounds.

As a rule, adult-onset diabetes can be well controlled with a balance of diet, exercise, and medication. If insulin is required, the patient must become accustomed to either giving his or her own injections daily or being dependent upon someone else to do so. Diet must be watched closely, and routine tests need to be done at home on the urine to ensure this balance. A fairly normal life can be maintained if the patient accepts his or her condition and takes appropriate care of himself or herself.

Many more people are alive today with heart disease because of medication and diet control than were just a few years ago. Emotional support of these patients in accepting the modifications and moderations in life-style is important on the part of the helping professional.

Asthma is a condition that can be triggered by a number of things. Different allergens as well as anxiety can cause bronchospasm in these patients. Usually this condition begins early in life. The patients tend to be very anxious individuals, although not always. If one could experience the smothering feeling that occurs with the asthmatic just once, one could better emphathize with the anxiety that having another attack brings about. Medication, avoidance of obvious allergens, and self-control of anxiety is a great deal of help to these patients.

It should be clear by now that in any disease process of a chronic nature, life-style modification is needed. Adaptation to this modification is in many cases a difficult experience. The difficulty has physical as well as emotional aspects. Family support is needed along with reassurance from the helping professional. Finally, before treating a patient with chronic illness and handicaps, the helping professional should make certain to acquaint himself or herself with physiological as well as the emotional factors involved.

Chapter 11

ON CRYING AND ASKING ADVICE

CRYING

UNFORTUNATELY, crying, particularly on the part of adults, poses a terrible threat to a large number of helping professionals. As a result, tears or their threat spoil more therapeutic sessions than can be imagined. A great many therapists simply do not want their adult clients to cry. Perhaps even more threatening is when the client is close to tears and unable to say anything. At this point, some therapists exert all of their energy on attempting to prevent the client from crying.

What can there be that is so terrible or overpowering about tears? Why should the helping professional feel so impotent when a client cries? Rationally, speaking, it is not the helping professional who caused the client to cry. Furthermore, it is not the helping professional who has inflicted pain or has been the cause of extreme unhappiness in the client's life. Rather, he or she is there for the purpose of helping the client.

The fast majority of clients who cry do so for personal reasons or because of personal experiences that have absolutely nothing to do with the helping professional. It is exactly for this reason that the helping professional or therapist has no rational basis for feeling responsible for the client's tearful condition.

Another reason why some helping professionals feel uncomfortable when a client begins to cry is the fear that the tears may never stop. However, this is an unrealistic and completely unfounded fear. The tears always stop and more often than not too quickly.

Crying can be an extremely therapeutic experience. Unfortunately many helping professionals feel compelled to prematurely rush in, offer reassurance, and stop the flow of tears.

More realistically, when a client appears to be close to tears, the therapist would be well advised to permit him or her to cry. However, this may not be a particularly pleasant or easy task for some helping professionals to do. Nonetheless, it is essential for clients to be permitted to cry themselves out. The resulting dividends are usually well worthwhile. This is so because after clients have cried sufficiently, they may feel a little guilty, but are also able to communicate more freely and openly about what is really bothering them.

I am reminded of a particular client who after crying for awhile was able for the first time to talk about a very painful tragedy in her life. Afterwards, she voluntarily explained why she was not able to talk about the tragedy "with those other people." She continued by saying ". . . every time I would try to talk with those other people, I would start to cry, and before I could get myself together, they would tell me not to cry because everything would be all right." In other words, the other helping professionals had unwittingly communicated disinterest or anxiety rather than understanding and concern.

Most often, it is best to reassure the client that it is OK to cry or to offer a tissue, sit back, and permit the tears to flow until they stop. This is particularly reassuring to male clients.

Two other important points about crying should be mentioned. First, crying or laughing at inappropriate times or events may be indicative of very serious psychopathology and should be treated accordingly. Second, crying can sometimes arouse feelings on the part of the helping professional, similar to that of a sympathetic mother comforting her crying child. Because these feelings appear to come on rather suddenly, helping professionals should be cautious and aware of this possibility when a client begins to cry. In essence, one need not be cold or callous, but should be empathetic as well as aware that sympathetic embracing will not help the client to talk about and to work through his or her problem.

What helping professionals would do well to realize is that crying is a healthy means of release and expression of feelings. For example tears are sometimes an expression of intense happiness and joy. At other times, tears may be a release and expression of frustration or extreme sadness. Furthermore, a certain amount of crying is sometimes necessary before one is able to verbally express and to discuss extreme emotions.

ASKING ADVICE

Every time I think of clients who ask for advice, I am reminded of what I was taught about the subject in my first graduate courses. Namely, under no circumstances was a helping professional supposed to give advice to clients with factual information.

Of course, this was partially so because of psychoanalytic and neoanalytic theories that were in vogue during this period of time. Since then, notions about giving advice have changed somewhat. However, one should still be cautious before quickly responding to client's requests for advice.

One reason for being cautious is well illustrated by two young newlyweds who came to see me for marriage counseling. They were having more frequent and more violent arguments. More specifically, though, each time they would go out to purchase something for their new apartment, the young bride always had difficulty making a decision and always insisted on being given her husband's advice about the color, brand, price, and so forth for everything they purchased. You guessed correctly if you assumed that the husband's advice always later in the day or week turned out to be wrong in his wife's final opinion. However, the purpose of this illustration is not to describe the young couple's problem but to point out what helping professionals may expect if they are too quick or eager to give advice. Moreover, this kind of experience may prove to be embarrassing for the helping professional and detrimental to the helping relationship.

Clients almost always come to see helping professionals for advice or information and for treatment. So too, treatment always involves giving information and sometimes advice. Thus, asking for and giving information and advice is a common interchange between clients and helping professionals. However, it may be helpful at this point to explain the difference between giving advice and giving information.

Advice always involves an opinion or value judgment on the part of the person who offers it. Advice also implies a suggestion as to something the client should or should not do. Information is the simple act of providing a client with access to knowledge that the helping professional has available to himself or herself. Obviously, information is considerably less risky than giving advice. However, every now and then, clients show up whose questions require a different approach from that which may ordinarily be used.

A client may abruptly ask questions: "Should a woman marry before completing college?" or, "Is it OK to spank a child?" These questions tend to be asked abruptly are out of context. They are often prefaced: "By the way . . . ?"; or, "This may not be important, but . . . ?" Then again, the questions may appear to be asked on behalf of someone else: "I have a friend who would like to know your opinion about . . . "; or, "It really doesn't matter to me, but my girlfriend would like to know . . . ?" The seriousness of their questions may also be glossed over with what appears to be humor: "My cousin said the funniest thing yesterday,"; or, (negative humor) "My mother is so crazy that she actually believes . . . . "

Nevertheless, what is important about these questions is not so much their content as their nature. The other important and common thing about these questions and/or statements is that they are usually expressions of hidden anxiety. Therefore, always consider that they may indicate that the client has a serious problem. They should also be handed accordingly and with the seriousness they deserve.

Another important thing is to remember that these types of questions should not be answered too hastily. This is because they rarely if ever contain sufficient information for the helping professional to formulate a rational answer. For example a client may abruptly ask, "Can mental illness be inherited?"; or, "Is it serious if a person experiences a memory lapse?" It would be a relatively simple matter to reassure the client that mental illness is not inherited or to say that a brief memory lapse is or is not serious. Further consideration would reveal that there is more to these questions than what is initially implied. Namely, what they probably mean is that these clients are seriously concerned about themselves or something they have personally experienced. Therefore, these questions should always be further explored with probing questions or statements such as "Tell me a little more"; or, "You are concerned about this?"

Another frequent occurrence is for clients to ask for advice when they have already made up their minds about it or when it may be impossible for them to follow the advice they may be given. Specifically, if advice provided by the helping professional is different from that which the client has already decided to do, it may prove to be more harmful than no advice at all. Basically, this kind of contradiction serves only to case doubt upon the client's predetermined course of action.

Most assuredly, to be asked for advice is one of the greatest kinds of compliments to be given. For this reason, many helping professionals find the temptation to be all but irresistible. This is especially understandable when the client prefaces his or her request with, "You are the only person I could possibly rely upon in this matter." This may very well be true because physicians, nurses, social workers, and other helping professionals alike do have awareness of certain knowledge and information not commonly available to other people. Nevertheless, the advice or information should only be provided after all of the related facts about the matter have been discussed and clearly understood. It is also of equal importance for the helping professional to make certain that what he or she has offered is clearly understood and that it is possible for the client to follow with what was suggested. To do otherwise would be an injustice to the client and may well prove to be harmful. The helping professional should also take care to not directly contradict or unwittingly demean advice that may have been given by significant others in the client's life. The only exception to this is when the helping professional is aware of precisely what is being contradicted and that, or she is certain that, it is incorrect. Also, helping professionals should not hesitate to tell clients that they do not know what to advise about certain matters that they are unfamiliar with or lack sufficient information to offer advice. In these situations, consultation or referral to someone with more expertise on the subject may be appropriate. In other circumstances, it may only require a review of current professional literature on the subject to be able to formulate an informed opinion.

Another important point is that helping professionals should always be cautious about questions relating to a client's sexual or family life. These questions are usually incomplete and consequently they frequently lead to awkward situations for both the helping professional and the client. For example I know a physician who was asked by a young couple if they should or should not have children. Their medical history clearly indicated that they should not. However, rather than simply providing the couple with this factual information, he explored the matter a little further. It did not take very much time for him to discover that the woman was approximately three months pregnant. It should be readily apparent that a hasty and seemingly correct answer to their question may have been disastrous.

In conclusion, helping professionals should never take their client's requests for advice too lightly. Rather, he or she should be careful to learn what their clients already know about the matter, from where or from whom they obtained their information, what they presently believe to be true, and what they may already intend to do regardless of what the helping professional may advise.

Chapter 12

GUILT, DEPRESSION, AND
THE SUICIDAL CLIENT

GUILT

WHEN confronted by a client's statement that he or she feels a lot of guilt, many helping professionals are too quick to offer reassurance and suggest that he or she should not feel guilty. The point is that the therapist may or may not be correct, but very little if anything has been learned about the particular circumstances that led to the client's reaction or what may be perpetuating the client's perceived need to feel guilty.

On one hand, guilt may well be a natural and normal part of the healing process. This is particularly so when a client is mourning the loss of a loved one. However, for further details about this matter, the reader is referred to the chapter on death, dying, and the bereaved relatives.

On the other hand, when a client is experiencing extreme feelings of guilt, or when the guilt has been present for an unusual amount of time, the matter certainly deserves further discussion, examination, and treatment.

In any case, the therapist would do well to encourage clients to talk more about their guilt before offering reassurance or anything else. For example I remember a woman who came to see me after having discussed her problem with another helping professional. She had explained to her other therapist that her husband had recently left her for another woman and that she felt extremely guilty about it. Apparently, the therapist quickly responded that she had no reason to feel guilty over what a "rotten so-and-so had done." Accordingly, she went on to explain to me that her previous therapist knew very little about her and apparently did not really care to know. In a sense, she was correct in her assessment. Namely, he was obviously in such a hurry to alleviate her of her guilt that he did not even provide her with an opportunity to tell her story. As a result, he lost a client and wasted his time as well as hers. Fortunately, I was able to encourage her to talk more about the matter, which by the way turned out to have nothing to do with her husband, who may or may not have been a "rotten so-and-so." Rather, her concern was that she had met another man at the office, so to speak, and felt that her friends and relatives would view this kind of behavior as being shameful since she had only been divorced for six months. Therefore, her problem was not guilt, but the fear that her friends and relatives might rebuke her for doing something she wanted to do. Further discussion also revealed that she was not certain of her own feelings about the matter.

Nonetheless, extreme guilt is usually based upon or a product of two things. First, it may be indicative of an unconscious wish. Second, at the cognitive level, it may be the product of irrational statements the client is making to himself or herself about some event or anticipated event. Ordinarily, these irrational self-statements contain some element of "I should have done . . . " and "I ought to be able to. . . . " However, the therapist's particular theoretical frame of reference should serve as his or her guide in determining the appropriate interventive measures to be utilized.

Whatever the therapist's frame of reference when the subject of guilt is mentioned, the temptation to offer immediate reassurance should be avoided. Rather, the client should be encouraged and permitted to talk more about it so that sufficient information can be elicited to determine the appropriate intervention.

DEPRESSION

Clients should be suspected of suffering from depression whenever they communicate that things are hopeless and they feel helpless to do anything about them. Also, it is not uncommon for a depressed person to unwittingly be directing a good deal of hostility toward himself or herself.

Other indications of depression are whenever a client is slow in responding and has little or nothing to say. The client may also demonstrate little or no interest in anything and complain of feeling tired most of the time. All communication on the part of the client is slowed, and you can expect their emotion to flatten.

The most common type of depression encountered by helping professionals is depression that has developed in reaction to a specific event that resulted in a loss by the client. The event could be the death of a friend or relative or the loss of a job. However, it should be emphasized that different events result in depression for different people, while other people appear to be left relatively unaffected. Fortunately, most clients suffering from reactive depression can usually identify the specific event or events to which they are reacting. Other types of depression may be of a severe psychotic nature, a precursor to some kind physical disease or a manic-depressive mood disorder.

Those depressions that are suspected of being organic or psychotic in origin should be referred for psychiatric medical evaluation. Moreover, nonmedical professionals would be well advised to do so whenever there is any question about this matter.

More specifically, when communicating with a client who is suffering from a reactive depression, there are certain fundamentals that are helpful. First, with the client's assistance, the helping professional should endeavor to determine when the client was last free from depression. Then, with a little direction, while moving forward in time, both the therapist and client can usually identify the specific event or series of events that led to the depression. Usually, when the event has been identified, brief cognitive and supportive therapeutic intervention soon relieves the client of depression, which is replaced with feelings of hopefulness and an increased level of activity. Furthermore, regardless of the helping professional's theoretical frame of reference, it is also helpful to challenge the client's illogical belief that he or she will experience the event and depression the remainder of their lives. This is the weakest link of the client's rationale for continuing to be depressed.

I remember a thirty-two-year-old women who had been suffering from reactive depression for approximately nine months. Her depression was in reaction to her husband's accidental death, which left her alone with a seven-year-old son. The client had pretty much convinced herself that she would be hopelessly depressed and lonely the remainder of her life and repeated again and again, "I can't stand it; I just can't live through it." Unfortunately, what the poor woman had not realized was that her life during the past nine months was living proof that she already had lived through her husband's death. Fortunately, once her irrational belief of not being able to make it was successfully challenged, she was able to participate in a self-help group for the recently single again, and upon last contact, was happily remarried. It should be pointed out, though, that she also received eight weeks of brief supportive therapy.

SUICIDAL DEPRESSION

Anytime a helping professional sees a depressed client, the possibility of suicide should be carefully considered. Unfortunately, there are no specific, guaranteed guidelines for helping professionals to rely upon in attempting to determine the degree of suicidal risk. Nonetheless, we do know a few helpful factors that appear to be related to suicide.

More to the point, the helping professional would be well advised to take very seriously any statement by clients that they are considering or have thought about ending their own lives. For example the author did a case study of 100 cases who had successfully or unsuccessfully attempted suicide. Findings revealed that 72 percent of the clients had revealed to their therapists or a relative, either verbally or in writing, their intention and thoughts about suicide. This same study also revealed that the vast majority of clients had communicated thoughts about death either to their therapists or a relative prior to their actual suicide attempt.

In another study, the author found that 42 percent of the 100 clients who attempted suicide had previously made the same attempt within the prior twelve months. Therefore, it would seem wise for helping professionals to check for previous suicide attempts when working with depressed clients. It stands to reason that if a client attempted suicide once, he or she has proven a potential for this kind of self-destructive behavior.

Other warning signals that should be seriously considered include clear descriptions of how the act is to be carried out, serious physical problems in conjunction with depression, and clients who exhibit delusional or psychotic behavior. Aged clients who are suffering from depression should also be considered a special risk for suicide. The reason for this is because older clients may be considerably less resistant to both physical and emotional problems than their younger counterparts.

In any case, the helping professional in all instances of depression should very carefully attempt to ascertain the suicidal risk. Unfortunately, one cannot expect to always be correct, but in most instances, close examination and conferences with supervisors and colleagues will usually reveal the extent of the risk so that appropriate precautions and treatment can be provided.

More specifically, as unpleasant as it may be, the helping professional should not hesitate or shirk the responsibility of discussing the possibility of suicide with depressed clients. Also, it should be emphasized that it is unlikely that the mention of suicide by the therapist will give the client any thoughts or ideas that were not already present.

Nevertheless, it is usually better to not just come right out and ask the client, "Are you planning to do away with yourself?" Rather it is more helpful and effective to gradually approach the subject with the client. For example you might begin simply by asking the client how things are going for him or her. Sometimes the response may yield only a shrug or a statement like, "OK, I guess," whereas with other clients the response may well be something like "I felt so bad that I sat on my bed for an hour last night with a loaded gun in my hand." Nonetheless, with clients who initially reveal little or no information, the therapist might say something like this: "Feeling kind of down?" Then moving progressively closer to the point, the therapist might say, "Things look pretty hopeless?" or "Seems as though there is little you can do about it?" and "Living seems to not be worthwhile?"

Unfortunately, even after approaching the subject of suicide with a client for a considerable amount of time, there is no guaranteed assurance that the client will not attempt suicide. For this reason, helping professionals would do well to carefully observe what the client's nonverbal communication may be suggesting. For example I remember a client who each time I progressively approached the subject would close his eyes, grimace, and shrug it off with a statement

suggesting absolutely no thoughts or intention of suicide attempts. Finally, because his verbal statements were so in-
congruent with his nonverbal expressions, I directly suggested, "It's just too painful to share such thoughts with
another person." He responded by saying, "You are damn
right! I sat with a bottle of pills on the table for two hours
before I came to see you and thought you would think I was
just another crazy nut." This provided me with the perfect
opening to reassure him of his worth and to enable him to
voluntarily admit himself to the hospital for rest, further
treatment, and evaluation.

Chapter 13

ON ANXIETY: THE CLIENT AND THE HELPING PROFESSIONAL

ANXIOUS CLIENTS

IT can safely be asserted that almost every client a professional sees is likely to be anxious at one time or another. This is particularly so during the first meeting. Nonetheless, it is not uncommon for some clients to not mention that they are anxious, and they perhaps may even insist that they are not.

On the other hand, if the level of anxiety is significant, it will be evidenced in some way. Moreover, anxiety during the first session is usually based upon two concerns: the presenting problem and wondering whether he or she will get along with the therapist. Regardless, there will always be a certain amount of anxiety during the first session.

Since the therapist must rely heavily upon the communication to help clients, it is important to promote an atmosphere that will be conducive to communicating with them. Most of the literature on therapeutic interviewing and communication skills emphasizes one or another way to organize the office or meeting area. However, I have found that organizing furniture and other objects in a manner that is comfortable for you is likely to be comfortable for your client as well. Nonetheless, it is very important and helpful in reducing anxiety during the first session to make every effort to prevent unnecessary interruptions, including extraneous noise. It has also proven to have been helpful to my clients to meet them outside of the office and offer a warm greeting and handshake. The passive and mysterious act of waiting in your office, while sitting behind a desk, can be very anxiety producing for your clients and should be avoided.

Conversely, you are not there to sell a used car. That is overdoing the greeting can also arouse anxiety. The purpose of the greeting is let the client know that you are a warm, genuine, professional person who is there to help.

More specifically, you might greet the client by saying, "Hello, I'm Joe Smith." Shake hands if the client responds and say, "Please have a seat where you feel comfortable." Following the initial greeting and introductions, it is sometimes helpful and productive to pause a few moments before saying anything else. The reason for pausing is to provide your client with the opportunity to begin talking if he or she is ready to do so. Finally, give the client your individual attention and studiously avoid taking any unnecessary notes.

What about those times when the client does tell you or behaviorally reveals that he or she is indeed anxious? Accordingly, as with other emotions, the therapist may immediately be tempted to tell such clients that they have nothing to worry about and to calm or sooth them before finding out what they fear. I have known a few students who attempted to calm these clients before they even had a chance to say they were anxious.

More specifically, there is nothing harmful about permitting clients to say that they are anxious or fearful. Also, there is no harm in telling an obviously anxious client that he or she appears to be anxious. Moreover, telling a tense, speechless, anxious client something like that frequently results in the client sighing with relief, nodding with agreement, and being able to talk freely about his or her feelings.

I remember one particular lady sat speechless and

trembling in my office. I remarked very caringly that she appeared to be upset about something. She responded by nodding agreement and while slightly sobbing, verbally poured her heart out. The important point about this example is that if I had prematurely attempted to calm her, she may never have been able to talk about and work through her fears.

Helping clients to recognize and talk about their unexpressed and sometimes unrecognized anxieties and feelings serves to reduce their insidious control and negative influence. Thoughts that are left unspoken can produce ideas and anxiety that are extremely threatening. This is because the same irrational thoughts that produce the anxiety are likely to be repeated and remain unchallenged. However, once they are put into words, the social worker can use them as a therapeutic tool by helping the client get in touch with their effect, identifying the upsetting things they are telling themselves, and challenging their rationality, which result in reduced anxiety. If what the client is telling himself or herself is based upon reality, the professional can help the client to mobilize personal and environmental resources and can do something about the problem.

On other occasions, the client may be totally unaware of what he or she fears, and the source of the problem may be linked with early life experiences. In these cases, the appropriate tentative diagnosis may be anxiety neurosis. An uncovering type of therapy may be beneficial and helpful to the client. In these cases, the foci should be upon attempting to bring to consciousness some of the unconscious factors.

I clearly recall a thirty-six-year-old man who suffered from an anxiety neurosis about homosexuality. During the uncovering process, the subject of homosexuality repeatedly came up directly and indirectly during several sessions. Wisely, the client's therapist avoided premature interpretations. Rather, he continued to listen attentively to the client's recollections of repeated struggles in breaking away from what he felt to be extreme constriction and domination by his father. The attentiveness and acceptance by the therapist promoted the development of a transference, which later made it possible for interpretation to modify the client's anxiety about homosexuality.

Perhaps the most important thing to be gained from this case illustration may be derived from the fact that the client described his initial presenting problem as being recurrent stomach acidity in reaction to his wife's not desiring sex as frequently as he. However, as early as the second interview, the client unwittingly revealed that he had experienced stomach problems since preadolescence. Fortunately, the therapist at once suspected that the client's problem was related to interpersonal relations in early childhood and thus decided to implement an uncovering type of therapy.

Another important thing for the therapist to understand is a particular kind of response to anxiety that literally results in tiredness and reduced resistance to disease. For example I remember a young man who became ill every time his parents planned to send him to summer camp. At the outset, this probably doesn't sound too serious, however, if you know anything about young boys, this is definitely not a typical occurrence. Nevertheless, what was happening was that the young man became so anxious over the thought of going to camp that he appeared to be depressed. However, what was really operating was that he was unable to express or to talk about his anxiety, which led to such decreased resistance to disease that he actually became physically ill.

Fortunately, after talking out his anxiety and excitement, which had previously remained unexpressed, he was able to attend the second half of summer camp without becoming ill.

However, not all anxiety should be viewed as being harmful to the client. Moreover, a certain amount of anxiety is conducive to the therapeutic process. Namely, an appropriate level of anxiety may be defined as existing when the level of anxiety is sufficient to motivate the client to make the effort required in a therapy session, but not to the extent of interfering with the client's ability to observe and talk about himself with the helping professional.

Learning to differentiate between normal anxiety and healthy involvement and abnormal anxiety and abnormal involvement is essential for the social worker. In understanding normal anxiety, it may be helpful to point out that human beings naturally tend to experience anxiety when confronted with something that is perceived as being threatening to them. Anxiety in these circumstances motivates the person to look beyond his or her vulnerabilities and to call upon other personal, and sometimes external, resources in order to reduce the threat. We experience normal anxiety whenever we face the unexpected and the unknown and whenever we experience growth or change. Accordingly, healthy involvement implies having the courage and assertiveness to do something about the situation.

Conversely, unhealthy anxiety is best understood in the person's abnormal involvement. That is rather than experiencing the fight or flight reaction, the person feels vulnerable and helpless to do anything about their situation. Therefore, in feeling helpless, the person tends to devalue himself or herself and to experience strong dependency needs.

In these cases, therapeutic intervention in indicated. However, the social worker would be well advised to recognize that in cases of acute anxiety and panic reactions, referral to a physician for medical and emergency treatment should be given careful consideration. In so doing, it is important to clarify the reason for the referral to the physician and to follow-up by requesting the physician's findings and recommendations.

In conclusion, the goal in communicating with clients is not to prevent anxiety. Rather, the appropriate goal would appear to be to enable these clients to experience less abnormal or unhealthy anxiety and to enable them to increase their capacity for changing and growing in the presence of normal or healthy anxiety.

ANXIETY AND THE HELPING PROFESSIONAL

Any consideration of anxiety would be incomplete if anxiety on the part of the therapist was neglected. Clearly, therapists are human and are fully capable of experiencing all the emotions and feelings their clients have. For some therapists, certain client mannerisms and problems tend to arouse anxiety in them. This can be a very painful experience and one that seriously interferes with the helping relationship.

Unfortunately, there are no magical or miraculous ways to avoid anxiety and the problems it may cause the helping professional. Moreover, each helping professional must learn his or her own way of handling anxiety; this is usually dependent upon the defense mechanisms most frequently used.

It may be comforting though to realize that your client will ordinarily be more anxious than you. Also, since anxiety tends to breed anxiety, it is usually productive to suspect a high level of anxiety on the part of your client.

A word of caution, though: Don't be too quick to tell your client about your own anxiety. Doing so may or may not result in your feeling better, but it is also an unreasonable burden to put on your client. Unfortunately, helping professionals too frequently give in to the temptation of talking too much about themselves. This is usually well intentioned and done to demonstrate to the client that he or she is not alone. However, this is rarely reassuring to the client and usually results in inhibiting the client from talking about himself or herself.

I remember a particular client who came to see me after having visited another helping professional. She began by explaining that the other doctor she had seen usurped most of her session by telling her about his personal problem that was similar to the problem she had presented. Her conclusion was to say, "In addition to all that, he had the gall to present me with a bill." So you see, in this case, the doctor not only inhibited the client from talking further about herself, but he lost the client.

Chapter 14

THE DYING CLIENT AND
BEREAVED RELATIVES

THE DYING CLIENT

DEATH is inevitably as much a part of life as anything else. However, except in cases of sudden accidents, death is more accurately viewed as being a process rather than merely an event. Furthermore, this process begins at birth, if not before.

The cultural influences on death and dying are important for understanding how the subject is viewed in our own society. For example, not too many years ago death among the Chinese did not represent an end, but rather some kind of reward by achieving the status of an honorable ancestor. This should not be too difficult to understand, though, as in any culture that is fraught with disease, pestilence, and death, the people become very familiar with death. Moreover, much of the mystery is removed, thus reducing reasons for hiding death.

Conversely, death is our society is hidden, denied, and above all avoided. Nonetheless, a recent trend toward making it possible for people to return home to die may serve to increase familiarity and reduce the reasons for hiding the death in our society.

Perhaps the most troublesome professional problem I have ever encountered was overcoming the difficulty in talking with patients who were dying due to acute trauma or from an incurable illness. Interviews with physicians about their feelings of helplessness to prevent the inevitable, their

100

decisions whether or not to tell their patients they were dying or when to tell them served only to further complicate matters. Unfortunately, there are no easy solutions to these problems, and accordingly, this would be possible only if the physician and the social worker simply cared less about what the dying patient may be experiencing and about what ultimately will occur.

Nevertheless, there are a few common sense and helpful notions that I have learned from experience, as well as the invaluable advice of a few esteemed colleagues. First, common sense suggests that it is important to assess the hard reality of the situation. Namely, it is important to determine whether or not the dying client has his or her affairs in order. For example you might determine from a relative if a legal last will and testament has been made, and you might want to inquire about other such business matters. Then, if these things are not in order, it is important to take the necessary action to permit and help the client to attend to them. Fortunately, this matter can usually be accomplished without bluntly telling the client that he or she is dying.

However, there remains the question as to whether the client should be told about his or her terminal situation. The final decision on this matter rests squarely with the attending physician. However, social workers, psychologists, and nurses are frequently consulted prior to arriving at a final decision.

Professional opinion about what to tell the client varies considerably. Namely, some feel that the client should be spared at all costs, or others may choose to ignore the question unless the client insists upon being told. Nonetheless, when possible and based upon my personal experience, it would appear to be far more humane for clients to be informed in order to permit them the opportunity of coming to terms with what is happening to them.

Fortunately, there is a growing body of knowledge on death and dying with which therapists should familiarize themselves. Specifically, therapists would do well to sensitize themselves to the needs of and coping mechanisms employed by clients who are dying.

Accordingly, the most important thing therapists can do is provide dying clients with the opportunity to talk about their needs and feelings in attempting to come to grips with the final act of life. Furthermore, it is very helpful for the therapist to accept the denial, hostility, and other common coping characteristics experienced and employed by dying clients. In so doing, it is helpful to rely upon the best listening skills available, and to permit the client to do most of the talking. Unfortunately, far too many professionals and nonprofessionals alike deny the dying person the right and dignity of talking about his experience. Most dying clients are very relieved to be able to talk about their feelings with someone who is a willing and supportive listener. The contrast serves only to further support a frequently unwitting, but destructive conspiracy of silence.

DYING CHILDREN

It never ceases to be a source of bewilderment that the most difficult things in life appear to be the most ignored. Unfortunately, the subject of dying children is no exception.

One of the most perplexing and heartbreaking realities of working with dying children is the nature of most common terminal illnesses among them. Namely, therapists are commonly assigned children who undergo treatment and later experience temporary remission, only for the inevitable cycle to painfully be repeated again and again for months and sometimes years. This is not intended to suggest, though, that children suffer from terminal conditions for much less periods of time.

Dying children I have known seemed to deal with the prospect of dying with less anguish than did their older counterparts. Simultaneously, their parents and close relatives appear to suffer more anguish over the death of a child than is experienced when older relatives are dying.

Without question, it is certainly more difficult to maintain a sense of objectivity with dying children than it is with older clients. Nonetheless, the social worker is well advised to guard against his or her own anger about the seeming unfairness of a child's death. While it is vastly important to the dying child to have someone who will be utmost with him or her through the entire experience, it is the of importance to recognize when you are unable to effectively deal with your own feelings about the matter. If the therapist is unable to maintain this level of objectivity, he or she runs the risk of having the child misinterpret his or her feelings of frustration and anger as being directed toward them.

As may be surmised from the above, working with dying children may be more personally difficult for any therapist. Nonetheless, children do appear to experience essentially the same phases of adjustment to death and dying as do older adults. Moreover, children also appear to adjust more readily to death and dying than do their relatives and parents.

BEREAVING RELATIVES

Traditionally, therapists have played a more active role with bereaving relatives rather than working directly with the dying patient. Nevertheless, working with bereaving relatives can certainly be helpful to the person who is dying.

For the person who dies, this is obviously the end of his or her life, but for others, the person's death does not necessarily constitute the end of his or her life. Moreover, faced with the death of a relative or friend, one experiences loss, but the actual adjustment to and acceptance of the loss is usually an extended and painful process that progresses gradually and not without a good deal of emotional conflict.

Perhaps the most important thing to recognize when working with a client who has lost a loved one is that it is their loss, the loss is real, and they should be provided the opportunity to grieve and to suffer their loss. Furthermore, we do know from scientific investigations that when a person experiences the loss of a loved one through death or some other reason, he or she also experiences certain mental processes, which require a reasonable period of time to work through. The phases, mental processes, and time are all necessary and normal components of the healing process.

One of the first things to expect from a bereaving relative is some kind of attempt, consciously and unconsciously, to deny that it has occurred. The relative may say "I can't believe it" or "He or she just can't be gone"; they may talk about the deceased person in the present tense and sometimes even take the deceased into account when making plans for the future. For someone who has not yet had this experience, this behavior sounds perfectly insane, however, it is a perfectly normal response to the situation. More precisely what this type of reaction amounts to is a relatively simple but straightforward attempt to hang on to the person who was lost.

Later, when the bereaved begins to face the reality of the situation, other things may be expected to occur. It is not unusual for the bereaved to feverishly carry out the wishes of the deceased, to identify in various ways with him or her, and to hang on to the deceased as a part of themselves. Moreover, memories of the deceased tend to become very clear and vivid; this is similarly a means of desperately holding on to the loved one.

All things being said, there is no easy way out of this for the grieving person. Although the experience of denial, hostility, bargaining, and final acceptance varies from person to person, everyone who is bereaved has a constant sense of sadness, helplessness, and hopelessness throughout the entire process.

On a related subject, a few words of caution would appear to be in order. It is not uncommon for clients to begin to cry when they are supported by the professional to ventilate their feelings. The act of crying can and most often is a very therapeutic experience for the client. Nonetheless, the therapist's emotional response may suddenly result in entrapment.

More specifically, tears tend to elicit feelings of pity or sympathy, and sometimes the impulsive act of taking the crying person into one's arms. Unfortunately, even though the act of embracing a crying client is intended solely as a source of physical and emotional support, it can suddenly arouse sexual feelings on the part of the crying client. This very thing became a source of embarrassment and led to a long and expensive process of litigation for a psychiatrist friend. Therefore, this cannot be too strongly emphasized, for these feelings of pity can also suddenly turn into very potent sexual feelings for the helping professional as well.

Perhaps the best response is for the therapist to allow the client to cry, to offer a tissue, and to sit back until the crying stops. This can be a very healing experience for the bereaving client and frequently results in him or her being able to conclude by constructively talking out and working through his or her intense feelings with the helping professionals.

BEFORE THE RELATIVE DIES

Social work intervention with a client who has a relative

that is dying is a very common occurrence. Moreover, the focus in these circumstances should be upon helping the client, and possibly other family members as well, to cope with their anticipatory grief.

Important matters for consideration when dealing with client's anticipatory grief is to recognize that family relationships are severely strained under these circumstances and even more so when the process occurs over an extended period of time. Economic problems, particularly with prolonged situations, are also a frequent source of stress for relatives.

Nonetheless, there are two specific things the therapist should make certain to focus upon when communicating with these clients. First, the therapist should help them recognize and accept their own feelings about the situation. For example it is not unusual for relatives of the dying client to overcompensate for their feelings of fear, guilt, and anger by literally exhausting themselves by caring for and assisting the dying relative. Even more troublesome for the client experiencing anticipatory grief is the feeling of anger toward the dying relative. Accordingly, the therapist is best advised to help the client deal with this openly and honestly. It is also helpful to reassure that this reaction is perfectly normal. Second, the therapist would do well to focus on helping the client to understand and accept that dying relatives frequently feel a need to talk about what is happening to them, perhaps even more than having so many things done for them. Fortunately, once the clients are able to allow the dying relatives to share their experiences, a great deal of the strain and resultant fatigue and anger quickly begin to dissipate for both. Even more important for the therapist to keep clearly in mind is to not neglect the needs of bereaving relatives, while helping them attend to those things that they need to do for the dying relative. In essence, bereaving clients are of little or no use to themselves or to others if they are not helped to maintain a certain level of physical and emotional well-being themselves.

BEREAVING CHILDREN AND ADOLESCENTS

It has been my experience that preadolescent children tend to require more time and experience greater difficulty in adjusting to the death of their mother than they do when the father dies. Additionally, children appear to adjust more readily to the death of a sibling than to the death of their mother or father. Conversely, it is not particularly unusual for certain children to adjust more readily to the death of a relative than do their parents.

Nonetheless, there are a few responses children and adolescents alike may generally be expected to have when a close relative dies. For example a number of children tend to regress and become more self-centered. I remember an eight-year-old youngster who suddenly began bedwetting when his father was killed in an automobile accident. Also something that added to his mother's chagrin was his insistence upon sleeping with her. I soon learned that the youngster felt a heavy obligation to take the place of his deceased father; however, the strain between wanting to be an adult and to be a child resulted in intermittent regression and bedwetting. Fortunately I was able to talk with the mother and to explain what was going on. I also stressed the importance of not hurting her son's feelings, but to inform him that she would be fine and to insist that he sleep in his own bed. This made it possible for both to share their feelings about their mutual loss. Also, convinced with brief supportive therapy, the youngster soon stopped bedwetting and was able to make a satisfactory adjustment to his father's death.

Generally, the therapist can be helpful in other ways. Perhaps the most important is to help the parents understand and deal with their own reaction and to emphasize the importance of not making any more changes in the home and family environment than may be absolutely necessary. During the following six months or so after the death of a parent, children need the reassurance of the routine previously afforded on a daily basis. Accordingly, parents should be encouraged to be appreciative of the child's attempts to be helpful with some of the household chores the deceased parent once assumed, but always admonishing encouraging children's feelings that they should attempt to replace the deceased parent. Also, the therapist should provide the opportunity for children to talk about and work through their feelings with someone who is a willing and supportive listener. In essence, children should also be allowed to mourn.

In summary, therapists are increasingly being called upon to play significant roles in death, dying and bereavement. This varies from casework and group work with the dying and bereaved, as well as educating other professional and paraprofessionals. Nonetheless, a great deal more needs to be learned about this subject, and counseling has a significant role to play in this endeavor as well.

Chapter 15

THE AGED CLIENT

HISTORICAL AND GENERAL CONSIDERATIONS

THERAPISTS have an important role to play in working with the elderly. Still, therapists all too often fail to view the older person as a full and appropriate candidate for intervention aimed at change, growth, and independence. Hopefully, the contents of this chapter will not only be helpful to you in more effectively communicating with older clients but also will help you to understand that what happens to the aged today may well predict your own future.

In recent years, demographic reports are revealing that people are living longer and increasing in numbers far more rapidly than ever before. This is particularly so for that segment of our population who are seventy years of age and older.

Unfortunately, a serious void currently exists in the professional literature that focuses on communication skills with specific respect to the latter years. Nonetheless, one of the most important contributions to the literature has been to develop a beginning body of knowledge for understanding the developmental stages of human growth when communicating with older clients.

Historically, older people in our society were largely perceived as being assets. Unfortunately, among other things, the post-Civil War years brought with them a considerably less than positive view of the elderly. However, more recent years have evidenced the acceptance of aging as being a legitimate concern for scientific investigation.

On a more positive note, the scientific investigation of aging has begun to produce a body of empirically based knowledge from which to more rationally understand the elderly. Accordingly, the importance of understanding the developmental stages when communicating with older people and other clients cannot be over emphasized.

STEREOTYPES

Anyone who desires to communicate meaningfully with older people must avoid stereotypes of the aging. This is true because all older people are not alike. Individual differences, particularly those that are cultural in origin, make it essential that the therapist be sensitive to and cognizant of the wide variety of life experiences and adaptations to the aging process.

While it is true that eventual decline is inevitable, the extent of such differs from individual to individual. Generally, these declines are evidenced through a lower efficiency in the cardiovascular system, impairment in the auditory, visual, and endocrine systems, and general physical decline. Unfortunately, in this society, the value of a person is largely based upon a person's productivity. Conversely, certain other cultures highly value the life experiences of older people.

The therapist who unwittingly connects human value or worth with productivity may also incorrectly equate the aging process with potential. Nonetheless, potential is a phenomenon that is difficult if not impossible to determine without first providing the resources, opportunity, and encouragement necessary for older people to realize in their later years.

Another common stereotype is the notion that "you cannot teach an old dog new tricks." What is even more unfortunate is that some older people accept this stereotype as though it were fact. More specifically, the therapists should be prepared to deal with resistance to change when confronted with an older client who holds such a mistaken belief. Additionally, other significant adults in the older client's life can and frequently do unwittingly discourage the older person from trying to grow, change, and achieve their individual potential.

Moreover, stereotypes of the aging usually focus on the physical, emotional, and social capacities of older people. Nevertheless, as distasteful as these stereotypes may be, they do appear to persist for social rather than individual reasons. Namely, the primary societal reason would appear to be to facilitate the transition of power and to make room for the young. In addition to advocating on behalf of older clients, the therapist can provide valuable assistance when communicating with the aged simply by helping them to recognize that these stereotypes have nothing personal to do with them or with their striving to realize their full potential during the latter years.

THE PHYSICAL SETTING

The physical setting is perhaps more important when communicating with older people than with any other age group. In some cases, it is best to see older clients in their homes, particularly if they experience difficulty in moving about. In other situations, it may be particularly helpful to have the older client come to your office. A specific reason for this is because many older people tend to isolate themselves unnecessarily. Therefore, having him or her come to the office is beneficial by getting the person out of the house and provides the older person with an opportunity to make a contribution to dealing with whatever problem they may have.

When seeing the older person in the office, a comfortable, well-lighted, cheerfully decorated room should be used. However, the helping person would do well to remain cognizant that many older people are quite sensitive to such things as temperature, noise, and light.

More specifically, the therapist should make certain that the room is adequately heated and should take precautions to prevent bright light from shining directly in the older person's face. It is also thoughtful to provide chairs of a comfortable height, which more easily facilitate rising and sitting. To be forced to request help in getting in or out of a chair is humiliating to some clients and may serve as another indicator to older clients that they are unable to care for themselves.

DIFFERENCES BETWEEN THE CLIENT
AND HELPING PROFESSIONAL

For the most part, the therapist is ordinarily younger than the aged client, and some are so much younger that the client may resent any attempt to communicate. This problem may be further aggravated when the social worker or someone other than the client has initiated the contact. There is also the possibility of the client feeling that somehow roles have been reversed and that he or she is no longer a parent figure but has suddenly become the child. An awareness on the part of the therapist that these feelings are likely to be present among older clients should go a long way toward more effective communication.

To further complicate matters, sweeping culture changes of contemporary society with respect to values, mores, and social problems suggest that older clients may well have been socialized in considerably different ways from younger therapists. Some differences in the physical ability of the client and the therapist may cause the older person to feel that the therapist cannot possibly understand them or their problems. In some situations this may well be true, but the therapist can help by guarding against perceiving the older person's problem solely based upon his or her own personal experience.

SELF-AWARENESS

Occasionally, therapists have special problems with their own feelings about aging and the elderly. For example the therapist may have ambivalent feelings about his or her own aging parents or may be middle-aged and anxious about the inevitable prospect of growing old himself or herself.

It is not uncommon for younger therapists to experience considerable difficulty in communicating with and relating to aging clients. The only solution to this problem is for the younger professional to adequately work through and resolve his or her own anxieties and feelings about the aging process. This particular point cannot be emphasized too strongly, for it is an absolute necessity for successfully communicating with aging clients.

PHYSICAL CONSIDERATIONS

An adequate understanding and awareness of certain common physical problems of old age is an absolute prerequisite for successful communication with these clients. Of particular significance is the realization that the majority of older people eventually experience some visual and hearing impediment. Therefore, therapists should very closely observe for nonverbal clues that may suggest one or both of these difficulties. This is especially important because some older people are reluctant to admit, much less volunteer, that they are unable to hear or see very well. Fortunately, if the therapist is alert he or she can usually ascertain whether the client is experiencing some auditory or visual problem. In any case, it may be helpful to speak more slowly and loudly than usual. However, you should be very careful because the older client may feel demeaned by overcompensation on the part of the helping professional.

Accordingly, it may also be helpful to reduce the length and pace of the session with some clients. This is particularly so if they appear to be overtaxed by the experience. Nonetheless, this should not be accepted as being universally true because many older people are very capable of prolonged, active sessions and may even enjoy them. For many older clients, communicating with their therapist serves as a meaningful outlet and constructive opportunity to talk about things that are important to them.

UNDERSTANDING SEEMINGLY OBNOXIOUS BEHAVIOR

Some older people are stubborn and outspoken and appear to have given up on the pleasantries of life. For some, this behavior serves as a defense mechanism that functions to protect them from further painful experience. Then again, they may have always been like this, and more than one study has demonstrated that stubborn and outspoken people tend to live longer and cope more adequately than do their seemingly more pleasant counterparts.

Frequently, these people are exasperating to the therapist. In these situations, extra patience and understanding is needed. Also, a realization of some of the reasons for this type of behavior should help the therapist to more appropriately work with these clients.

Another behavior that is frequently interpreted as being

troublesome is the older client's tendency to reminisce. However, nothing could be further from the truth. Far from being troublesome, reminiscing can serve as an invaluable source for obtaining historical information and data for assessing personality changes. Reminiscing may also serve as a valuable therapeutic opportunity for the therapist to help older clients to work through old problems and to reassure them that their life has been both valuable and worthwhile.

At times, older people exhibit behavior that may be misinterpreted as being obnoxious, unthoughtful, and perhaps even asocial. Nonetheless, reassessment of the behavior as to the motivation behind it would serve to facilitate communication between the older person and the therapist.

More specifically, interrupting conversations and pushy behavior that inconveniences others can be attention-getting devices. For example continual complaining as to service delivery in restaurants can also be a way of increasing one's feeling of self-esteem and importance. This behavior should be dealt with on a mature level and not responded to as if to admonish the individual for this behavior. Remember, if there is one aspect we know about human behavior it is that people tend to respond as they have been responded to. If one is treated in a childish manner, one tends to respond with similar behavior.

Yet one should be reminded that the elderly are individuals, and indeed they are as uniquely different as anyone else. The seemingly obnoxious behavior is a mistaken way for many to be recognized as being unique as well as worthwhile human beings. Unfortunately, this behavior, when misinterpreted, often tends to elicit admonishing and or condescending response; then the older person feels rebuked. What the therapist must learn to do is to look behind as well as beyond this type of behavior being emitted by older people so as to understand the true meaning of what is being communicated.

OTHER CONSIDERATIONS

By now, it should be clear that the more awareness you have of your own feelings about aging, the more effective and comfortable you will likely be when talking with older clients. It is also helpful to speak audibly and distinctly, to avoid the use of slang expressions, and to permit the client to reminisce.

Moreover, both your appearance and attitude are important to most older clients. Also a comfortable and appropriate environment is helpful, and continuous close observation for nonverbal clues to the older person's physical and emotional health should be made. In conclusion, older clients are individuals who have the right to the same individual considerations that the clients of any age should be accorded.

INDEX

A

Acceptance, 26, 32, 35, 41, 42, 44, 50, 59, 61, 63, 96
Adolescents, 40-46
  and stability, 40-43
  troubled, 46
Advice, 9, 35, 45, 69, 81-85
Affection, 26, 61-64, 81, 105
Aged, 109-116
  reminiscing, 115
  stereotypes, 110-111
  and suicide, 90
Amputation, 75-76
Anger, 25, 29, 31, 35, 50-51, 57-60, 88, 102
  masked hostility, 60, 61
  and therapist, 50-51, 57-60
Anxiety, 17, 26, 27, 28, 48, 49, 74, 83, 93-98
  neurosis, 95, 96
  physical exacerbations, 78, 96
  in preverbal child, 17, 18
  productive, 95, 97
  therapist's, 13, 32, 42, 62, 79, 98-99
Arthritis, 76
Asthma, 78

B

Basic Considerations
  and fundamentals, 5-12, 40, 48, 57-58, 65, 70-71, 104-110
Bereaving, 76, 86, 103-105
  children, 107-108
  relatives, 103-106
Body image
  altered, 73, 75-78
Burn patient, 75

C

Children, 13-39
  abuse-neglect, 48, 51, 58
  anxiety, 17, 18, 26, 27
  anger, 25, 30, 31, 34, 35
  birth order, 26
  fear, 23, 24, 27, 28, 29, 30
    of strangers, 15-17, 20, 31-32
  of two to four, 20-23, 37, 38
  of five to seven, 20, 23-25, 35, 36, 38
  of seven to eleven, 25-26, 35, 36, 38
  play therapy, 23, 35
  preverbal, 13-19
    development, 14-19
      motor, 14-19
      psychosocial, 15, 17, 18
    talking with, 13, 14, 18, 19
  separation from parents, 27-30
  time, 7, 23
  unique language of, 14, 21, 22, 23, 27, 34-39
Chronically ill patient, 70-75, 77, 78
  and family, 70, 72, 75, 77, 78
Clarification, 9, 10, 21, 61
Confidentiality, 10, 11
Confronting, 69
Continuing Education, 12, 52, 70, 78, 85, 102
Crying, 27, 28, 32-33, 79-81, 105

D

Death, 77
  and relatives, 51, 52, 103-104
Deductive reasoning, 38
Depression, 88-92, 96
  psychotic, 88, 90
  reactive, 70, 73, 88, 89
  suicidal, 89-92

117

Diabetic patient, 77
Divorce, 51, 52, 87
Dying client, 100-103, 105
  child, 102-103
  (*see also* Bereaving)

E

Ellis, Dr. Albert, 59
Empathy, 49, 81
Enable, 49
Expressions
  eyes, 7
  facial, 7, 17, 61
  (*see also* Nonverbal communication)

F

Fear, 30, 31-32, 42, 43, 44, 48, 57, 72

G

Greeting, 94
Guilt, 25, 31, 49, 50, 60, 68, 70, 76, 77, 80, 86-87

H

Handicapped patient, 70, 72, 75-76
History of client
  psychosocial, 48, 49, 66, 70, 89, 115
Honesty, 48
Hostility (*see* Anger)

I

Incongruities, 80, 92
  in communication, 8, 11, 34, 82-83
Information, 25, 43, 69, 82-84
Instructions
  to client, 9, 10, 47, 48, 51, 68, 82-84
Intensive Care, 75
  syndrome, 75
Interpretation of client, 9, 10, 21, 37, 65, 83, 91-92
  preverbal child, 13-14
Interventive strategy, 5, 6

L

Language, 40, 67
  syncratic and cryptic, 34-36, 37
  (*see also* Children, unique language of)
Listening skills, 7-9, 80, 86, 87, 94, 96, 98-99, 102

M

Masterbation, 43-46
Maultsby, Dr. Maxie, 59
Mental deficiencies, 51, 65-69
  arithmetical skills, 67
  behavior with, 65-66
  vocabulary in, 43
Mourning (*see* Bereaving)

N

Noise, 93, 112
Nonverbal communication, 7, 13, 14-17, 27, 28, 34, 35, 36, 61, 72, 91, 92, 113-114
Note taking, 7, 94

O

Objectives, 6, 48
Office, 20, 21, 72, 74, 76, 93, 111-112, 113-114
Open-ended questions, 9

P

Parents, 19, 29, 30, 31, 32, 46, 47-53
  fear, 48, 49
  guilt, 49, 50, 68, 86
  with mentally deficient child, 68-69
  single parents, 52-53
  step-families, 51-52
  uncooperative, 48-51
Patience, 37
Personal appearance
  dress, 7, 20
Positive regard for, 53, 61
Probing, 24, 37, 59
Prejudice, 58, 59

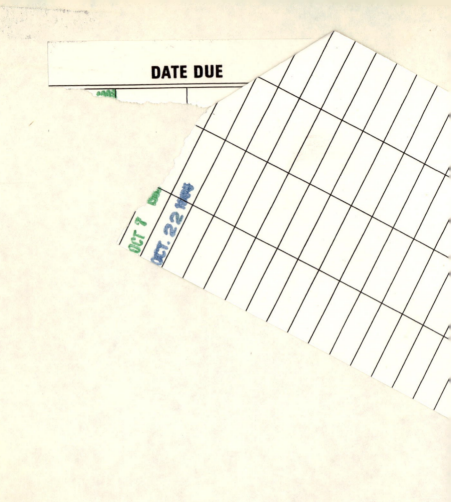